FORD

SMALL-BLOCK ENGINES

How to Build Max Performance

Jim Smart

CarTech®

CarTech®

CarTech®, Inc.
6118 Main Street
North Branch, MN 55056
Phone: 651-277-1200 or 800-551-4754
Fax: 651-277-1203
www.cartechbooks.com

Edit by Bob Wilson
Layout by Connie DeFlorin

ISBN 978-1-61325-802-6
Item No. SA546

Library of Congress Cataloging-in-Publication Data Available

Written, edited, and designed in the U.S.A.
Printed in China
10 9 8 7 6 5 4 3 2 1

All photos are courtesy of author Jim Smart unless otherwise noted.

DISTRIBUTION BY:

Europe
PGUK
63 Hatton Garden
London EC1N 8LE, England
Phone: 020 7061 1980 • Fax: 020 7242 3725
www.pguk.co.uk

Australia
Renniks Publications Ltd.
3/37-39 Green Street
Banksmeadow, NSW 2109, Australia
Phone: 2 9695 7055 • Fax: 2 9695 7355
www.renniks.com

Canada
Login Canada
300 Saulteaux Crescent
Winnipeg, MB, R3J 3T2 Canada
Phone: 800 665 1148 • Fax: 800 665 0103
www.lb.ca

CONTENTS

Acknowledgments 4
Introduction 5

Chapter 1: Building Basics...........9
Getting Organized 9
The Physics of Power 11
Giving Away Power.....................14
Building a Stroker 15
Assembly Technique 16
The Mock-Up 17
Checking Endplay......................17
Thermostat............................18
Dynamic Balancing 18
Common Sense Block
    and Head Prep 18
How Much Is Too Much? 19
Ford Muscle Parts 19

Chapter 2: The Block..................20
Boss 302..............................23
351W..................................24
Buying a Used Block 26
Aftermarket Blocks:
    Iron or Aluminum?.................26
Ford Performance 27
Dart Machinery 29
Speedmaster 30
BMP...................................30
Budget Blocks.........................32
Block Preparation.....................32
Fasteners and Clean Threads....34

Chapter 3: Rotating Assembly ..35
Crankshaft 37
Crankshaft Selection 39
Stroker Kits..........................40
Building a Stroker 42
Strength in Stud Girdles 42
Connecting Rods 43
Aftermarket Connecting Rods.44

Piston Selection 45
Harmonic Dampers
    and Flywheels.......................47
Dynamic Balancing 49

Chapter 4: Lubrication 50

Chapter 5: Cylinder Heads........56
255: The Misfit..........................60
1968 302 Tunnel Port 60
Boss 302................................60
Aftermarket Cylinder Heads ...62
Ford Performance Cylinder
    Heads...............................62
Dart Machinery 63
AFR 64
Edelbrock 66
Head Work 68

**Chapter 6: Camshaft
and Valvetrain 70**
Camshaft Function....................71
Street Camshafts 73
Dual-Pattern Camshafts 75
Racing Camshafts 75
Why Degree a Camshaft?.........76
Timing Components 77
Lifters 77
Pushrods and Rocker Arms 78
Valve-Spring Pressures.............80
Spring Height 81
Valvetrain Geometry 82
Rocker-Arm Adjustment..........82

Chapter 7: Induction.................85
Carburetor Selection.................86
Carburetor Size 91
Carburetor Spacers...................92
Intake Manifold 93
Bolt-on EFI...........................95

EFI Throttle-Body Sizing 96
Fuel Injectors 97
Supercharging
    and Turbocharging..............98
Nitrous Oxide 99

Chapter 8: Ignition..................102
Spark Knock 104
Breaker-Point Ignition...........104
Dwell Time 105
Electronic Ignition 105
Ignition Coils........................106
Distributor 107
Ignition Wires.......................110
Spark Plugs 111
Charging System 111
Starters...............................113

Chapter 9: Exhaust...................114
Exhaust-System Sizing............114
Secondary Tubes
    and Collectors....................117
Equal-Length, Step,
    and Tri-Y Headers 117
Exhaust System Selection 119
Stainless or Aluminized? 122
H-Pipes and X-Pipes 123

Chapter 10: Engine Builds....... 124
Budget 347 Stroker.................124
Carroll Shelby's 427W 127
Race-Ready Raptor 427W 131
5.0L High Output 136
Street 302 Tunnel Port 138
Supercharged 347 Stroker.......141
5.0L Turbo Power 142

Source Guide 144

ACKNOWLEDGMENTS

I've been working in automotive journalism for more than four decades. I've managed to take a passion for automobiles and turn it into a career. By pure dumb luck, I stumbled into this business when *Mustang Monthly* editorial director Donald Farr gave me my dream shot, which was to write about Mustangs for a living. Donald invited me to jump into the editor's chair to take over for him so that he could launch *Popular & Performance Car Review* (later *Muscle Car Review*).

At the time, I thought, "What the heck do I know about being an editor?" I was scared to death. I had a lot to learn at the time—not only about writing and editing but also about people and how to get along. Becoming a journalist didn't come easily, and I've hit my share of potholes (some self-induced) along the way. Suffice it to say that I didn't get here without a lot of help from true friends who have become extended family. We've all managed to ride this incredible tide together.

This book didn't happen without help from people in this industry—friends who put their lives and jobs aside to help with this book and previous books. They've supported me through untold thousands of magazine articles and projects. Summit Racing Equipment, Comp Cams, Holley, Edelbrock, Ford Performance, National Parts Depot, Crane Cams, Crower, and a host of others have come to my rescue through the years.

A wealth of local talent has been eager to help as well, including JGM Performance Engineering, Valley Head Service, MCE Engines, L&R Engines, Trans Am Racing, Burbank Speed & Machine, Lykins Motorsports, Full Throttle Kustomz, Mustangs Etc., and untold others around the country. My extended family has become a large one.

Writing automotive technical manuals has never been easy. A tremendous amount of research is involved along with the burning of midnight oil. It is very time consuming and risky at times because information is always changing. What is true today may not be true tomorrow or next year. Information becomes dated amid proof that there's a better way. Every honest technical writer fears bad information ending up in their work. It has happened to me, and it has surely happened to others.

With that being said, a lot of research has gone into this book. It is the result of a lifetime of working with seasoned engine builders, racers, and car builders. I've taken what I've learned from these professionals and incorporated their approaches into books, web articles, and magazine articles. Sometimes, I want to say, "Don't shoot me—I'm the messenger!" because readers perceive that I am an engine builder. Although I have built engines (most of them Ford) through the years, I haven't practiced this profession daily in decades.

My job is to take what engine builders teach me and turn it into editorial content. Put 50 engine builders in a room, and you will get 50 different opinions regarding how to build an engine. No one who reads this book is going to agree with everything in it. I invite your constructive comments on how this book's content can be improved so that I may continue to serve you better.

INTRODUCTION

Ford has a proud legacy of great American V-8s. For 22 years, Ford produced the flathead V-8, which was introduced in 1932. It was a simple, no-nonsense V-8 engine that remained in production while the rest of postwar Detroit was developing powerful overhead-valve (OHV) V-8s. It remains a very popular and nostalgic mill today. The flathead led to Ford's Y-Block V-8, which was introduced in 1954 and was an overwhelming success.

Ford product planners and engineers began to see the need for a more advanced V-8. The Ford-Edsel (FE)–series big-block V-8 was introduced in 1958 and was produced through 1976 for a wide variety of Ford and Mercury car lines, including the Ford GTs that produced wins at Le Mans. There was also the Mercury-Edsel-Lincoln (MEL) big-block V-8 for the Lincoln and Thunderbird in 1958, which was a smooth high-torque powerhouse that was used mostly in the Lincoln Continental through 1968.

As Ford turned its attention to more economical volume-selling automobiles, such as the Falcon, Comet, Fairlane, and Meteor, planners looked to a smaller, more lightweight pushrod V-8. This lightweight gray-wall iron approach was

The small-block Ford debuted in 1962 as the "90-Degree Fairlane V-8," displacing 221 and 260 ci. The 289 arrived for 1963 with a larger 4.000-inch bore and the same 2.870-inch stroke. For 1965, the 289 4V "Premium Fuel" engine got a boost in compression and had 225 hp (compared with the "Regular Fuel" 289 4V that had 210 hp prior to 1965).

When Carroll Shelby performed his Mustang magic in the fall of 1964, the GT350 fastback was born. Shelby gave the 289 High Performance V-8 a more radical mechanical camshaft, Cobra high-rise intake, 715-cfm Holley carburetor, Tri-Y long-tube headers, and the cast Cobra T-pan underneath. The result was 306 hp at 6,000 rpm.

Ford introduced the 302-ci small-block Ford in 1968 to replace the 289, which was phased out that year. The 302 had the same 4.000-inch bore as the 289 yet with a 3.000-inch stroke. This engine is in a 1972 302-2V with a changed appearance and "Power by Ford" valve covers, which first appear in 1968.

Beginning with the 1977 model year, all Ford engines were fitted with a lightweight aluminum air cleaner. Performance was all but dead at the time with a focus on fuel economy and emissions. This engine is in a 1979 Mustang with 5.0L-2V (302 ci) power.

applied first to the 144- and 170-ci inline 6-cylinder engines in 1960 for the Falcon and Comet. It was then applied to a new small-block V-8 for 1962.

221, 260, and 289

The all-new redesigned Ford Fairlane and Mercury Meteor for 1962 led to a new featherweight V-8 known as the "90-Degree Fairlane V-8," which displaced 221 and 260 ci. We know it today as the small-block Ford. In 1963, Ford found greater displacement in the 4.000-inch-bore 289-ci V-8 with a 2.870-inch stroke. In 1968, the stroke was increased to 3.000 inches to get 302 ci. In 1985,

the 302 became known as the 5.0L High Output with roller tappets.

When the Fairlane V-8 arrived, it had a 3.500-inch bore and a 2.870-inch stroke (221 ci) as well as a version with a 3.800-inch bore and 2.870-inch stroke (260 ci). This short stroke reduced piston speed and frictional loss issues and was coupled with a high-revving capability. The larger bore, which would grow to 4.000 inches the following year, allowed for generous valve sizing and breathing. Few can dispute the runaway success of Ford's small-block V-8. It wound up in dozens of racing venues around the world and continues to be campaigned successfully more than a half century later.

351W

As the rest of Detroit developed midsize V-8s that displaced 327 ci to 400 ci, Ford found itself in the uncomfortable position of being behind the competition. Despite that, Ford was forging ahead behind the scenes to develop a more muscular midsize V-8 that was later named the "Cleveland," which displaced 351 ci. However, Ford needed a quick answer for 1969. It took the 289/302–based small-block and raised the deck 1.280 inches to achieve 351 ci by using a 4.000-inch bore and 3.500-inch stroke.

The 351W (Windsor), a 5.8L V-8 engine, was a quick fix for the midsize V-8 crisis. The 351C (Cleveland), which was still in development, wouldn't be ready until the 1970 model year. Ford was able to develop and build the 351W on short notice and mounting pressure from the marketplace. What Ford didn't know at the time was that the 351W would be the midsize mainstay for decades.

The 351C was conceived to replace the small-block 302/351W V-8s, with displacements ranging from 302 ci (Australia) to 400-plus ci in North America. The 400, which was introduced in 1971, was a raised-deck version of the 351C that was developed to replace the dated 390 FE big-block in full-sized Fords and Mercurys. It is also true that Ford never called the 400 the "400M." The 351M (Modified) engine was the only M-series Cleveland ever made, according to Ford engineer Bill Barr, who headed up the Boss 302 program.

Ford Australia embraced the 351C, also producing a 302-ci version of this broad-shouldered Ford V-8 with a 3.000-inch stroke, 4.000-inch bore, and even smaller

This 351W-4V engine is fitted with the Buddy Bar Casting C9OX-9424-A dual-plane intake manifold, which was available in a number of different forms from Shelby and from Ford. George Parker of Virginia restored this 1969 Mustang GT SportsRoof and opted for the C9OX intake and Autolite 4300 carburetion with the Hi-Po air cleaner to clear the hood.

Cleveland wedge chambers. Ford North America learned that the 351C (100 pounds heavier) was not a suitable replacement for the small-block V-8 and dropped this engine after 1974. The 400 remained in production through the late 1970s. Ford de-stroked the 400 to 3.500 inches to conceive the 351M.

302 Tunnel Port

Despite Ford's great success in road racing, it conceived a real dud in its 1968 302 Tunnel Port engine for Sports Car Club of America (SCCA) Trans-Am competition. Although the Tunnel Port had worked well with the FE Series 427-ci big-block, it was a major flop for the 302-ci small-block.

The issue wasn't the Tunnel Port's ability to make power, it was the RPM range that it had to operate at to make real power. That RPM range (8,500 to 9,000) was too high for these engines to stay together even with a bolstered four-bolt main block. Racing greats, such as Parnelli

Jones and George Follmer, who were chasing Camaro and determined to win, blew up Tunnel Ports all over the country suffering unacceptable losses. Ford engineer Bill Barr went to work on a solution, and Ford staged a comeback in the 1969–1970 season.

Boss 302

Ford's short-lived Cleveland-head Boss 302 engine, which was produced

for 1969–1970, was a unique chapter in Ford engine history. The Boss story began with the troubled 1968 302 Tunnel Port V-8 that was conceived for SCCA Trans-Am competition. Ford's 289-ci small-blocks performed very well in Trans-Am competition until the Camaro arrived in 1967. Mustangs had a hard time keeping up with 302-ci Z-28 Camaros, which produced wins across the country.

Ford chief engineer Bill Barr acted quickly to find a solution. He knew that the 302 head casting could not accommodate the needs of a high-revving small-block. He visited Ford Advanced Engines and looked at the new 335-series engine (351C) that was being developed. He looked at the bore and head-bolt spacing, which were identical to the 289/302/351W. He learned that with the right pistons and rods, he could put the 351C cylinder head on top of the 302 block. He just had to modify the cooling-system passages and develop the right pistons. Then, the 302 could make peak horsepower at 7,500 rpm to spank Camaros.

The Boss 302 came out of the gates with large valves, petite wedge chambers, and high-dome forged

The short-lived 302 Tunnel Port was a 1968-only engine that was built strictly for SCCA Trans-Am competition. Because these heads made peak power well above 8,500 to 9,000 rpm, they failed with great regularity. They just couldn't catch Camaros at 7,500 rpm. (Photo Courtesy Lykins Motorsports)

The Boss 302 engine for 1969–1970 was something of a hybrid small-block of the 289/302 family that used 351C-4V heads that were modified for the 289/302–based block. The Boss 302 block, which began in 1968 as the Tunnel Port block, was a four-bolt-main casting with thicker main webs and decks.

This Boss 302 engine is in Trans-Am trim with a pair of Dominators and a road-race pan. It is obviously more powerful than its street counterpart.

pistons ready to take on the competition. For 1969, the Boss 302 was a bit too aggressive for street performance. For 1970, Barr felt that the engine needed to be tamed more for street use to where it made better mid-range torque (better drivability) with smaller valve sizing.

5.0L High Output

Ford reinvented the 302/5.0L small-block in the 1980s with the introduction of the 5.0L High Output engine in 1982 and then the High Output roller-tappet block in 1985. Not only was this block designed for roller lifters but it also sported thicker main webs, decks, and cylinder walls for durability. Ford changed the 28-ounce offset balancing to a 50-ounce offset in 1982, which allowed for heavier connecting rods in the High Output 302 engine. Sequential electronic fuel injection (SEFI) came in 1986.

The 5.0L High Output small-block Ford that was introduced in 1986 was a radical change because it was unlike anything that had ever been produced.

Its induction system looked more like a vacuum-cleaner attachment than an intake manifold. It had long intake runners that were engineered for better low- to mid-range torque. The 5.0L's appearance didn't change much until 1994 (on the redesigned SN-95 Mustang GT).

Saleen Mustangs with the 5.0L engine had a unique induction system with better breathing and an improved appearance.

BUILDING BASICS

Engine-building technology has made huge strides over the past half century. Better cams, heads, induction, and ignition are available. This provides a better playing field on which to build a small-block Ford. Every engine project needs a blueprint—a plan. Plan out your engine build before ordering parts and securing a machine shop. A large part of building an engine is knowing what you can afford and not ordering more than you need.

The radical nature of a lumpy cam will get on your nerves in stop-and-go traffic. There will never be enough intake manifold vacuum to run the power brakes and climate control. There are strictly street engines, weekend bracket-racing engines, and all-out racing engines. An engine for the street and weekend bracket racing works well if you can achieve a comfortable balance.

Getting Organized

Perform the engine teardown where you can catalog all of the parts and keep them properly stored until it is time to use them. Keep engine parts and fasteners in jars or plastic containers that have been labeled

This is what you can expect when searching for a good core. Look for evidence of a rebuild before buying. Good, untouched cores are hard to find. Mic the cylinder bores. If they're 4.040 inches in diameter, move on. Never overbore beyond 4.040 inches. Sonic check the cylinder walls while you're at it for thickness.

with a marker. Take the block, heads, crankshaft, and connecting rods to a reputable machine shop immediately upon disassembly. This avoids any confusion and keeps your project moving.

If you do not have time or cannot afford a machine shop at the time, leave the engine assembled

until you can. I speak from experience because too much is lost both mentally (information) and physically (parts) after the engine has been disassembled and months pass. Take plenty of photos during disassembly.

Avoid engine assembly on a windy day because it generates dust. Any kind of stray matter (dust or dirt), no

Small-block Fords in the 1960s and 1970s have an engine manufacture date code stamped into the block deck above the timing cover. "5C4R" is this 289's build date code for 1965/March/4th. This date code also includes the letter "R," but its meaning is unknown.

On the bottom of the block above the starter is the casting date code and Ford casting number. "C5AE-6015-E" indicates that this is a 1965 289 block. The casting date code of "5C2" means 1965/March/2nd, just two days before the engine was assembled on March 4, 1965. A circled "C" on the block indicates the Cleveland foundry.

When disassembling an engine, its state of health will become apparent. Examine the bearings, cylinder walls, piston rings, and piston skirts for wear issues and reasons for failure. The goal is to eliminate issues that caused the excessive wear or engine failure.

This is a 1966 289 High Performance V-8 from a Shelby GT350. These intake gaskets and heads have evidence of oil ingestion into the ports from the lifter valley. This engine was burning oil but not from bad rings or valve seals. It was drawing oil from the valley into the intake ports, which would cause smoking from one or both banks.

All block plugs and fittings must be removed before cleaning begins. Oil gallery plugs, freeze plugs, and coolant drain plugs must be removed to allow cleaning access to the block's most intimate spots.

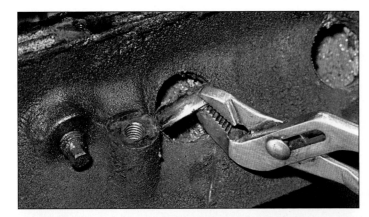

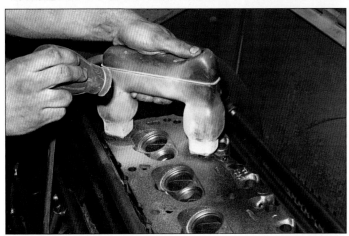

Magnetic particle inspection can find cracks in castings.

Don't be surprised to find freeze plugs inside the water jackets. I've found engines with chronic overheating issues that had additional freeze plugs inside the water jackets. This happened at Ford with new engines, and it happens with mass-production rebuilders. Inspect cooling passages for debris.

Thermal cleaning appears to be the most environmentally responsible casting cleaning. Castings are cooked at 400°F and then blasted with abrasive media (steel shot) to make them like new. A final shakeout removes all of the steel shot.

matter how small, will cause engine damage. Use only lint-free tack rags (static cloths) for wipe-down. When it is time for assembly, everything should be in proper order. Pistons should be numbered and matched to each bore for dynamic balance. This means that each bore should have been checked with a micrometer and honed to the piston's specific size. All piston rings should be individually gapped for each bore.

Lay out all of the engine's critical parts on the workbench in proper order. You will never regret taking your organization to the extreme. Number each cylinder with a felt-tip marker at the block deck. Lay the pistons and rods on the bench in cylinder-number order.

Because the Ford castings in the

Main-bearing saddles should be inspected for evidence of spun bearings and oil starvation, especially if there's been a catastrophic failure. These grooves were machined into the saddle at the factory for bearing security.

1970s have a reputation for flaws, be cautious when selecting yours before committing. If you buy a salvage-yard core, get a written money-back guarantee. First, inspect the potential core for obvious issues: leaks, cracks, overheating, voids in castings, and poor workmanship. Never overbore

a small-block Ford beyond 4.040 inches.

The Physics of Power

We've long been led to believe that horsepower is what "power" is all about. However, horsepower is

Always Use a Torque Plate

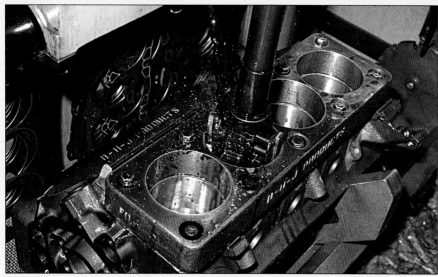

Cylinders are finish-honed using a torque plate for consistency. Your machinist must use a torque plate, which simulates cylinder-head installation with the bolts properly torqued.

Does your machine shop use a torque plate during cylinder honing? If not, find another machine shop.

A torque plate simulates cylinder-head installation by getting the block where it would be with the heads installed and bolts torqued. The reason for this is to simulate the installation of the cylinder heads on the block when the machinist is honing the bores. You want cylinder walls dimensionally where they would be with the heads installed. If you hone a block without a torque plate and then bolt on the cylinder heads, cylinder-wall dimensions change as the bolts are torqued.

rooted more in Madison Avenue advertising rhetoric than fact. In the power picture, horsepower doesn't count for much, especially on the street, where you need good low- to mid-range torque. Torque (and when it is available) is what counts. Torque is the grunt that gets the car going, and horsepower is the force that keeps the car moving.

Engines do their best work when they reach peak torque. When an engine is below peak torque, it has more than enough time to completely fill the cylinder with air and fuel. When engine RPM rises above the torque peak, there isn't enough time to completely fill the cylinders with air and fuel, which is where real power comes from.

The power that is felt from an engine is torque multiplied by engine speed (RPM) to produce a number that tells us something about the engine's output. This theory dates back to an inventor named James Watt, the inventor of the steam engine. Watt's theory was simple. It compared the work that his steam engine could do with the same work that an equal number of horses could do. Watt determined that a single horse could pull a 180-pound load a distance of 181 feet in the time of 1 minute. This formula resulted in 32,580 ft-lbs per minute.

Watt rounded the formula to 33,000 ft-lbs per minute. He divided this figure by 60 seconds, which

Lifter bores are honed for stability and oil control. Not enough machine shops do this. Ask your machine shop to do it.

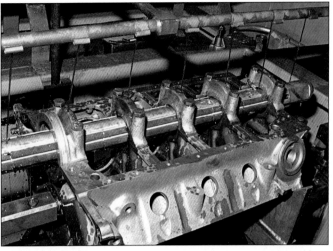

Main-bearing saddles are align honed for trueness and improved bearing crush and security.

All bolt holes should be chased to clean up the threads.

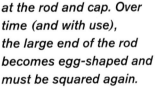

Stock connecting rods are reconditioned by milling the mating surfaces at the rod and cap. Over time (and with use), the large end of the rod becomes egg-shaped and must be squared again.

Once the rods and caps are milled, the rod assembly is honed (as shown) to get the journal perfectly round again. Rods may also be shot-peened for added strength.

resulted in 550 ft-lbs per second and became the standard for 1 hp. As a result of Watt's calculations, horsepower has become a measure of force in pounds against a distance in feet for the brief period of 1 minute. Then, we take this formula and apply it to an engine's crankshaft at each journal throw to arrive at horsepower. This is based on the number 5,252.

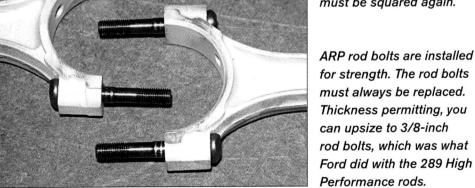

ARP rod bolts are installed for strength. The rod bolts must always be replaced. Thickness permitting, you can upsize to 3/8-inch rod bolts, which was what Ford did with the 289 High Performance rods.

Torque and RPM are divided by 5,252. Torque and horsepower always intersect at 5,252 rpm. If you can solve this equation at 5,252 rpm, RPM cancels out, ultimately leaving horsepower equal to the torque figure. In fact, if you work this out on a graph, the torque, horsepower, and RPM lines should always intersect.

When torque is looked at by itself, it is the measure of an engine's work. Horsepower is a measure of how quickly the engine does the work. Torque mostly comes from displacement and stroke. This means that the real power that is derived from an engine comes in the torque curve when torque ramps up to peak torque. The broader the torque curve, the better the power package.

A broader torque curve comes from making the most of the air/fuel mixture across a broader RPM range. This is best accomplished with a longer stroke and a larger bore. Strokers are about making the most torque across the broadest range.

Giving Away Power

When you're planning for power, builders rarely stop to consider how power gets wasted in an engine's execution. Friction is the power pickpocket that is hiding inside of the engine. Most of the friction occurs at the pistons and rings. Some gets lost at the bearings and journals. However, more is consumed at the piston wrist pins, lifters and bores, cam lobes and lifters, rocker-arm fulcrums, valve stems, and valve guides.

Your objective needs to be a compromise between having tolerances that are too loose and too tight. Piston-to-cylinder-wall clearances are critical to having good cylinder sealing but not too much friction that

Compression rings are installed using an expander. Not all machine shops use an expander. Some shops just roll them on. With whatever approach you use, keep ring distortion to a minimum.

Ring end gaps must always be checked even if you've purchased pre-gapped rings.

there is a loss in power. The same is true for rod and main bearing clearances. You want liberal clearances (for good oil flow and heat transfer) and less friction.

Another power-robbing issue is engine breathing. You want an induction system that helps your engine breathe well in the RPM range for which it is designed and built. This means choosing the appropriate intake manifold and carburetor. If you go small on carburetor sizing, breathing is limited. If the size of ports don't match, breathing is restricted. If you opt for cylinder heads where port sizing is too limited for the displacement, breathing is restricted.

This small dot on the compression ring indicates the orientation, meaning that the side with the dot faces up. Don't get this backward.

On the exhaust side, you want good scavenging that makes sense. Long-tube headers aren't required for great breathing. Shorty headers do the job without the shortcomings of long-tube headers. If the header size is too large, torque is lost. If the header size is too small, power is reduced on the high end. The exhaust system has to work hand in hand with the heads, camshaft, and induction system.

Building a Stroker

A stroker is an engine with an increased or decreased stroke. By increasing an engine's stroke (the distance that the piston travels in the cylinder bore), displacement is gained. Short-stroke engines perform well at high RPM, where they make the most horsepower and torque. The focus here is about increasing the stroke to achieve greater amounts of torque and horsepower.

Stroking an engine does more than just increase the displacement. It increases torque by giving the engine a greater mechanical advantage. When the stroke is increased, the engine's crankshaft arm, or lever, is increased, which makes the most of a combustion cycle. The longer the stroke, the greater the torque.

Increasing the rod ratio via a longer rod improves piston dwell time at each end of the cylinder to get more power.

The stroke comes from the length of the crankshaft's rod-journal arm. Then, that length is doubled to find the engine's stroke. The length of the crankshaft's arm is doubled because we get that arm in two directions: top dead center (TDC) and then bottom dead center (BDC). This is a simple 2:1 ratio. Take the crankshaft arm (measured from the crankshaft centerline) and double the measurement. If the arm is 1.5 inches, you have a 3-inch stroke.

How is additional power gained from a stroker? It is due to the greater mechanical advantage of a longer crankshaft arm, but there's more. The cylinder is also being filled with a greater volume of air and fuel, which provides more power all by itself. From the stroke and cylinder swept volume, we can determine torque. Torque is the truest measure of an engine's power output.

When considering the crankshaft's arm, the distance from the crankshaft centerline to the center of the rod journal, this is where torque is born. Torque is that physical pressure at your backside when the accelerator is pressed. So, what exactly is torque? Think of the crankshaft's arm as a simple lever, like you were taught in high-school Physics class. Torque equals the downward force of the stroke multiplied by the length of the lever or arm.

If you take a 351's 400 ft-lbs of peak torque, this means that each cylinder bore is producing 740 pounds of pressure on each power stroke. Torque is increased when the length of the arm is increased. When the length of the arm is increased, the stroke is increased.

Despite the advantages of a stroker, there are disadvantages as well, especially if you're determined to pump the most displacement possible into a small-block Ford. When you stroke the 302 or 351 to its limits, you lose piston skirt, which hurts stability. You also push the piston pin into the piston ring land area, which weakens the piston's design. It also puts the pin close to the piston dome, which exerts too much heat on the pin and boss.

Rod length is also important. When we haul that piston deep into the cylinder bore, we are also bringing it closer to the crankshaft counterweights, which can create conflict. This means that you need a longer connecting rod to get the piston down there without interfering with the counterweights.

Sometimes, you can find off-the-shelf connecting rods to complete your stroker. However, you may be forced to custom fabricate connecting rods that will work. The more expensive stroker kits have custom parts, such as rods and pistons. More

Attention to detail is vital when building a stroker. Do a mock-up first using engine assembly lube at the journals to where you can turn the crank and observe clearances. Install the number-1, number-3, and number-5 main caps snug, but not tight. As you rotate the crank, check the crank counterweight and rod journal clearances as they relate to the block.

affordable kits have off-the-shelf parts that make the kits possible without expensive tooling costs.

Assembly Technique

I will provide methods and practices that work for professionals who do this every day. When it comes to assembly practices, engine building professionals stress two main areas: 1) cleanliness and 2) double-checking your work. Never assemble an engine in the same area where it was torn down. Even minute amounts of dirt, dust, or grit can stop an engine cold by scoring bearing surfaces and cylinder walls.

I stress double-checking your work because this approach saves time. If you think it's inconvenient to check your work two or three times, consider the inconvenience involved in a teardown because there's high oil consumption or having to collect the pieces of a blown engine because something critical was missed during the assembly process.

The easiest way to make power is to raise compression. However, you don't want too much compression. The compression ratio depends on your plan and the fuel that is available. Another quick way to unleash power is to have less internal friction. Internal friction can be reduced with roller tappets; a double-roller timing set; and lightweight, full-roller rocker arms. However, there are other ways, such as using more liberal clearances and lightweight components. This is a balancing act because you also want durability, good oil pressure, and low oil consumption.

There are many misconceptions regarding cam treatment during assembly. Molybdenum grease (known as moly lube) is used only on flat-tappet cam lobes, never on the journals or roller-tappet lobes. Moly lube is productive in the work-hardening process during camshaft break-in during the first firing and running the engine at 2,500 rpm for 30 minutes. Assembly lube is used only on the cam journals.

Billet ring compressors make light-work of assembly. However, they are expensive and limited to one size. For home use, you want an adjustable ring compressor for a variety of bore sizes. The piston and rings should be bathed in either 30-weight engine oil or an assembly lube that has been specifically engineered for rings and cylinder walls.

No Leaks

Gasket technology and engine sealing have made major strides since the small-block Ford was introduced. Fel-Pro is the only gasket brand that I use, although there are those who prefer to use other brands. Excellent gaskets are available. Help your gaskets work better by using The Right Stuff from Permatex in areas that could become compromised, such as between rear main seal halves at the block and the main cap.

Jeff Latimer, a respected engine builder whom I work with, discourages staggering the rear main seal tips away from the main cap and block mating surfaces. He believes that the seal tips can be compromised (bunched) in the number-5 main cap and leak.

The Mock-Up

Savvy engine builders begin assembly with a mock-up phase, where the bottom end is assembled and lubed without piston rings and checked for proper clearancing throughout. A mock-up allows you to check critical clearances all around. This means rods and journals must be checked to make sure they're going to clear the bottoms of the bores and piston skirts. At a minimum, you must have at least 0.0100 inch of clearance between every rod and the block. Be careful how much iron is ground away because you risk going all the way through into a water jacket or the world outside.

Checking Endplay

When checking the crankshaft endplay, don't forget to check camshaft endplay as well. Endplay needs to be conservative to keep timing chain tracking safe. Too much endplay hurts longevity and can cause engine failure via connecting-rod side movement.

As the cylinders are stuffed, check the freedom of rotation each time that you fill a cylinder. If there are any issues, you will feel this with the troubled bore. Don't wait until all eight pistons are installed to find out that the crank won't turn or to discover that there's a lot of resistance.

Crank and cam endplay are crucial clearances that must be checked. Check crank endplay during the mock-up phase in case any additional machine work has to be performed to achieve proper fitment.

Once the short-block is assembled, true top dead center (TDC) must be checked before degreeing the cam. If true TDC isn't correct, nothing else will be correct. Set the dial indicator (as shown) at the block deck and zero the gauge. Slowly move the piston to TDC. Zero the dial indicator at the highest point on the piston dome. Slowly turn the crank and observe needle movement. Slowly bring the crank back to TDC in the opposite direction and observe needle movement to the same amount. Turn the crank back to TDC.

Dynamic balancing is mandatory for any engine build because it is important for smoothness and durability.

Whether you install a new cam or reuse the old one, degree the cam and note the numbers for your permanent record.

Thermostat

Run a high-flow water pump along with a 180°F thermostat. Stay away from a 160°F thermostat, which makes the engine run too cool. Never run your Ford small-block without a thermostat. If you are running an engine-driven fan, go with a Flex-A-Lite flex fan or a factory thermostatic fan clutch for efficient cooling. The fan must be halfway into the shroud for the best results. Always use a fan shroud for improved air velocity through the radiator.

Dynamic Balancing

Every small-block Ford build should include dynamic balancing in the interest of durability and smoothness. Dynamic balancing is nothing more than getting reciprocating mass to the same exact weight

as the crankshaft counterweights. Each piston, ring, rod, and rod bearing is placed on a gram scale and weighed to the lightest individual reciprocating-mass assembly. Remove material from each piston and rod to get everything down to the same weight as the lightest. Then, spin the crank on a balancer to determine whether weight needs to be added or subtracted to the counterweights.

Because small-block Fords are externally balanced, both the harmonic damper and flywheel (or flexplate) must be included in the balancing process. Small-block Fords that were produced prior to 1982 are 28-ounce offset balanced, whereas those from 1982 onward are 50-ounce offset balanced.

Common Sense Block and Head Prep

During the machining process, get all of the machine work out of the way at the same time. This is the time to chamfer all of the oil-gallery transition points to reduce oil turbulence and improve flow. Chamfer the oil drainbacks in the valley to improve drainback. Install drainback screens to keep foreign matter out of the pan. Eliminate stress risers in the castings to reduce the risk of cracking.

Another positive modification is to machine the block and to use a one-piece rear main seal, which virtually eliminates the risk of rear-main-seal leakage. The number-5 main cap and saddle are

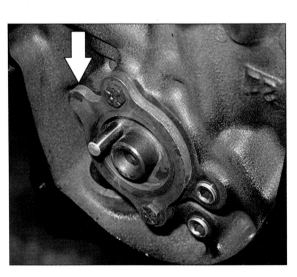

Confusion abounds regarding small-block Ford cam retainers. There are two basic types: early and late. The early type uses countersunk screws and a spacer along with a corresponding cam sprocket (prior to 1965). This is a post-1964 cam retainer, which uses bolts. The dog ear (arrow) channels oil to the distributor gear via a passage in the cam retainer and block.

The factory oil gallery plugs are pressed in. Replace them with screw-in oil gallery plugs. Your machine shop can do this.

Instead of using the stock oil-pump drive-shaft, use the ARP pump shaft, which improves durability. Do this even for stock applications.

Where the head gasket meets the intake manifold and heads, apply a thin bead of Permatex's The Right Stuff to prevent oil leakage.

bored together to eliminate the two-piece-seal grooves. The crank's number-5 journal lip is machined off to where it looks like a 1982–up 5.0L crankshaft journal. Although I've seen machine shops use oil or assembly lube on these one-piece seals, it has been suggested to me to never use any lubricant on the seal lip or the crank in this area. You can actually cause an oil leak by lubricating the lip.

How Much Is Too Much?

Something that I regularly see is the liberal use of RTV silicone sealer in engine builds. Remember that there's a minute gap between components when you bolt them together. There's a gasket there to prevent leakage. There is absolutely no need to pile on sealer in addition to the gasket, especially if you're using modern gasket technology.

One-piece silicone oil pan and valve cover gaskets do not require sealer. You may use tiny applications of sealer where castings come together (leaving a potential void), such as at the intake-manifold gaskets or where the pan joins the timing cover. However, excessive amounts of sealer can break away and fall into the oil pan or block cooling passages.

I've seen globs of cured sealer in oil pickups and in cooling passages, limiting oil and coolant flow.

Ford Muscle Parts

In the early 1970s, Ford released two supplements to its original *Muscle Parts Story. Supplement #1* was on parts interchange and description. One chapter is dedicated to the 90-degree small-block V-8 (221/260/289/302 ci). The next chapter is committed to the 351W V-8. These chapters included technical data for each engine type, including detail on the design and engineering elements of major components, such as the block, heads, induction, crankshaft, connecting rods, and pistons. The intent was to get enthusiasts familiar with Ford's lightweight small-block V-8s. These are helpful publications

It is easy to go overboard with gasket sealer. Don't do that. Only use a thin film of The Right Stuff around cooling passages and only use it along the bottom of intake ports to allow for the irregularities of head, block, and intake manifold angles, which can lead to vacuum leaks.

to have on hand, especially if you're building a period engine and are seeking authenticity.

THE BLOCK

When Ford introduced the small-block engine, it was thinking about strength. The goal was to make a rugged, well-thought-out, light-weight casting that could take some punishment and still have room for growth. The 1962–1963 221-ci and 1962–1964 260-ci engines have five-bolt bellhousing blocks with either a 3.500-inch bore (221) or a 3.800-inch bore (260).

Casting numbers are C2OE, C3OE, or C4OE. These casting numbers are in different locations depending on the block casting. In 1962, block casting numbers were cast into the rear lifter valley rail on top. In 1963–1964, they were cast just above the starter. Casting date codes in 1962–1964 were cast in the block just above the starter. These blocks are easy to spot because their 3.500-inch and 3.800-inch bores are noticeably smaller than the standard 4.000-inch bores on the 289 and 302.

Block deck cooling passages on the 221 and 260 are triangular shaped as well, which makes them different from the 4.000-inch-bore 289 and 302. Early-1962 221 and 260 blocks had two 1½-inch freeze plugs on each side, which later changed to three freeze plugs in 1963 with the

The timeless 221/260/289/302 block didn't change significantly until 1985, with the advent of roller tappets and more robust block architecture. The 289/302 block was cast in two foundries: Cleveland (CF) and Windsor (WF). It appears to be that the earlier 221 and 260 blocks were cast exclusively at the CF foundry.

arrival of the 289. These early blocks are also identified via engine-mount bolt-hole spacing, as the earliest 221/260 blocks were 5.940 inches apart along with two freeze plugs, instead of the traditional three that are most often seen. Revised engine-mount bolt-hole spacing (to 7.000 inches) happened in the 1963 model year to reduce noise, vibration, and harshness (NVH).

The 289-ci engine entered

This is a new old stock (NOS) 260 block with a five-block bellhousing pattern that was common from 1962–1964. All 221 and 260 blocks have the five-bolt bellhousing pattern. The 289 block was produced in the five-bolt pattern (through July 1964) and six-bolt pattern (from August 1964 through the 1990s).

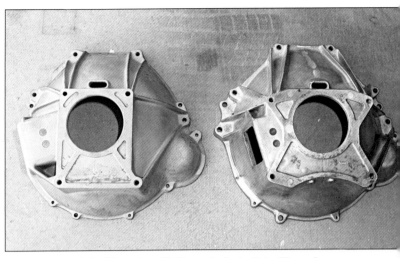

The five-bolt bellhousing (left) and six-bolt bellhousing (right) are shown. In the summer of 1964, Ford changed to a six-bolt bellhousing to reduce noise, vibration, and harshness.

All block casting numbers and date codes are cast into the block just above the starter on the right-hand side. The alphanumeric date code confirms the actual date that the block was cast. A stamped date code is the date that the engine was manufactured. This casting date code of "5G26" indicates that this is a service replacement block that was cast on July 26, 1965.

This is the back of a 289 High Performance engine block with the "HP" marking and orange paint dab, which is the color code for a 289 High Performance block. The wider main caps make it a Hi-Po block (not the block itself).

production in the 1963 model year. It had a five-bolt bellhousing bolt pattern just like the 221 and 260 along with the 7.000-inch mounting bolt holes and three freeze plugs on each side of the block. Five-bolt bellhousing 289 blocks have casting numbers of C3OE, C3AE, C4OE, C4AE, and C4DE.

Beginning with the 1965 model year (August 1964), Ford revised the 289 block to a six-bolt bellhousing bolt pattern to reduce NVH. The block casting numbers are C5AE and C6AE. The 289 High Performance V-8 had the same block as the 289-2V and 289-4V, with the exception of wider main bearing caps, such as is found on the Mexican blocks.

Standard 289-2V and 4V main bearing caps are 15/16-inch wide at the block's main saddle, and they taper as they rise to the top at the casting and cap numbers. The wider 289 High Performance main-bearing cap is 15/16-inch wide at the block and does not taper. It is a wider cap for its entire height and width. The Hi-Po rule applies to both five- and six-bolt-bellhousing 289 High Performance blocks.

The 302 block appeared for the first time in the middle of the 1967 model year in 289 applications with

The 289 High Performance engine block has wider main caps than is seen with standard 2V/4V engines. The standard main cap tapers from the block to the top of the cap. The Hi-Po main cap is the same width across the entire cap. Orange paint also helps to identify this cap.

Mexican blocks can also be identified by their Ford casting number: C8AM 6015-B. The "2280" is undoubtedly a date code. The casting also shows that it was cast in Mexico.

Ford cast 289/302 blocks in Mexico, which are identified by these two round bosses that protrude from the front of the block along with wider main caps. The wider main caps are also an asset of the Mexican block.

Mexican blocks, such as this one, employ wider main caps, which is similar to the 289 High Performance main cap. If you can find a Mexican block that is not salvageable, you can get the main caps for your build. However, these main caps and your block will have to be align bored/honed for compatibility.

Beginning in 1982, Ford went to a single, one-piece rear main seal on the small-block Ford. Here are the two blocks side by side. The 1982–up one-piece rear main seal is on the left, and the two-piece rear main seal (1962–1981) is on the right.

a C8AE or C8OE casting number and a "302" in the valley. The aspect that made the 302 block different than the 289 was 0.019-inch-longer cylinder skirts to accommodate the 302's longer 3.000-inch stroke. It is not uncommon to find a 1967–1968 289 engine with a 302 block.

The 302 block evolved in the years following 1968 and had casting revisions that are worth mentioning.

While most of these blocks are interchangeable, with 289 types dating back to 1965, it is important to note that the clutch-equalizer-shaft pivot boss on the left-hand side was eliminated from the 302 block beginning in 1975. This means that you need a bolt-on clutch-equalizer-shaft pivot bracket for a 1975–up 302 block if you're running a manual transmission and the classic Z-bar clutch linkage.

As a rule, casting and engine build date codes should fall within 30 to 60 days of your Ford's build date if it is fitted with the original engine. An example is "5A26" (January 26, 1965) which notes the year, month, and day of casting or manufacture. If the date code is cast into the block, it indicates the exact date that the block was cast. If it is stamped into the block, it indicates the engine's exact date of engine assembly.

An example of a casting number is "C5AE-6015-E" for a 289 block.

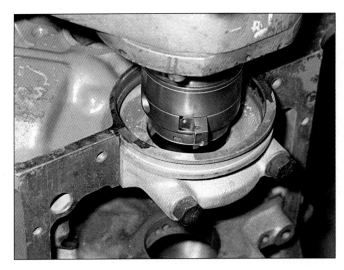

Look for these numbers because they will help you choose the correct block. If you find a matching number block with cylinder bores that have been bored to 4.040 inches or larger, the block can be sleeved by a qualified machine shop and returned to service. The cost to sleeve a block is approximately $100 per cylinder. The good part about sleeving a used block is that it has seasoned iron from steady cycling of heating and cooling over time. However, sleeving is discouraged if you're going racing because, no matter what anyone will tell you, sleeving provides less stability than the iron bores have.

Check any block that you're considering for cracks and severe deck warping before machine work is performed. This process can be accomplished by any qualified machine shop before expensive machine work begins. Weak spots are generally around the deck near cylinder-head bolt holes, cylinder bores, and main saddles.

Mexican 289/302 blocks are believed to have a higher nickel content, but this has never been true. Mexican blocks and their north-of-the-border counterparts

A 221/260/289/302 block with the two-piece rear main seal can be converted to use a one-piece seal. Cut the number-5 rear main journal (as shown) for a one-piece rear main seal (1982–up). Any qualified machinist can do this, which should eliminate any leak issues.

they weigh the same, which debunks the high-nickel-content theory. Nickel adds weight to an iron casting.

The aspect that makes a Mexican 289/302 block more rugged is its wider 15/16-inch non-tapered main-bearing caps like were used on 289 High Performance blocks. Mexican blocks are a good source for wider main caps where you can find them. If you use them on another block, have a machine shop measure and line bore/hone them to the proper size.

Boss 302

Ford's limited-production 1969–1970 Boss 302 engine block is highly sought after for its four-bolt main caps, heavier main webs, thicker decks, and screw-in block plugs. With fewer cores being available today, it isn't racers who will be competing with you to purchase these blocks. Instead, it'll be restorers who are looking for authentic date-coded Boss blocks.

Based on extensive research, five basic Boss 302 block castings were produced: C8FE, D0ZE-A, D0ZE-B, D0ZE-C, and D1ZE-B. C8FE is the 1968 302 Tunnel-Port block that was also used in some production 1969 Boss 302 Mustangs and Cougars. The most common Boss 302 block castings are the D0ZE and D1AE. The D1ZE-B is a Ford replacement service block. Because Boss 302 engines failed primarily due to piston skirt failure, plenty of service blocks are available.

As with the earlier 221, 260, 289, and 302 blocks, the maximum

This is the 1968–1971 Boss 302/Tunnel Port block (Tunnel Port for 1968 only) with four-bolt main caps, thicker webs and decks, and screw-in freeze plugs.

The Tunnel Port/Boss 302 block has screw-in freeze plugs.

The 351W's bottom end is virtually the same as the 289/302/351C. The exception is that the 351W has a larger main journal size of 3.000 inches, compared to the 289/302/351C's 2.249 inches.

This is something that you don't see every day: "C8FE-6015B" with a casting date of "8M5," which means December 5, 1968. Although this block came out of a June-1969-production 1969 Boss 302 Mustang and was assembled in the summer of 1969, it is a 302 Tunnel Port block. Unused Tunnel Port blocks wound up in production Boss 302 Mustangs.

The 351 Windsor (351W) block sports a taller deck height than the 289/302, which is where its displacement is increased. It is easily identified by the increased deck height and the reinforcement gussets at the front of the block. The 351W block was produced in two different deck heights: 9.480 inches (1969–1971), and 9.503 inches (1972–up).

overbore for the Boss 302 block is limited to 4.040 inches. It is suggested to overbore no greater than 4.030 inches, especially if you intend to take the engine to 7,000 or 8,000 rpm. Have the cylinder walls sonic tested for thickness. Like the rest, you can sleeve a Boss 302 block for about $100-plus per cylinder and go back to a standard bore. A Boss 302 block is worth saving.

351W

The 351-ci Windsor block has a taller deck and additional gussets in front (on top), which makes identification easy because you're dealing with a wider block. The 351W has a 1-inch-taller deck to accommodate the increased 3.500-inch stroke. Based on my abundance of experience with these engines, I believe that

1969–1971 351W blocks are stronger than those that followed. Blocks that were cast in the 1970s have a reputation for cracking or having manufacturing flaws in the casting.

The 351W had a long production life, which means that many blocks are available for the taking. Overall, the 351W is a very hardy casting that a lot of power can be infused into without spending a fortune.

Block Identification: 221, 260, 289, Boss 302, and 351W

Displacement	Model Years	Casting Number (6015)	Part Number (6015)	Bore Size	Deck Height	Information
221 ci	1962–1963	C2OE-G	C4OZ-B	3.500 inches	8.206 inches	5-Bolt Bell
221 ci	1962–1963	C3OE-A	C4OZ-B	3.500 inches	8.206 inches	5-Bolt Bell
260 ci	1962–1964	C3OE-B	C4OZ-B	3.500 inches	8.206 inches	5-Bolt Bell
260 ci	1962–1964	C3OE-C	C4OZ-B	3.800 inches	8.206 inches	5-Bolt Bell
260 ci	1962–1964	C4OE-B	C4OZ-B	3.800 inches	8.206 inches	5-Bolt Bell
260 ci	1962–1964	C4OE-D	C4OZ-B	3.800 inches	8.206 inches	5-Bolt Bell, 7.000-inch Mounts
260 ci	1962–1964	C4OE-E	C4OZ-B	3.800 inches	8.206 inches	5-Bolt Bell, 7.000-Inch Mounts
289 ci	1963–1964	C3AE-N	C4AZ-B	4.000 inches	8.206 inches	5-Bolt Bell
289 ci	1963–1964	C4OE-C	C4AZ-B	4.000 inches	8.206 inches	5-Bolt Bell
289 ci	1963–1964	C4OE-F	C4AZ-B	4.000 inches	8.206 inches	5-Bolt Bell
289 ci	1963–1964	C4AE	C4AZ-B	4.000 inches	8.206 inches	5-Bolt Bell
289 ci	1963–1964	C4DE	C4AZ-B	4.000 inches	8.206 inches	5-Bolt Bell
289 ci	1963–1964	C3OE-B	C4OZ-E	4.000 inches	8.206 inches	5-Bolt Bell, High Performance
289 ci	1963–1964	C4OE-B	C4OZ-E	4.000 inches	8.206 inches	5-Bolt Bell, High Performance
289 ci	1965–1967	C5AE-E	C5AZ-E, C5OZ-D, C7OZ-C	4.000 inches	8.206 inches	6-Bolt Bell, from 8/1964
289 ci	1965–1967	C5OE-C	C5AZ-E, C5OZ-D, C7OZ-C	4.000 inches	8.206 inches	6-Bolt Bell
289 ci	1965–1967	C5AE-E	C5OZ-D	4.000 inches	8.206 inches	6-Bolt Bell, High Performance
289 ci	1965–1967	C6FE-A	N/A	4.000 inches	8.206 inches	289 Race Block, GT40
289 ci	1965–1967	C6AE-C	N/A	4.000 inches	8.206 inches	—
302 ci	1968–1969	C8OE-A	D1TE-E, D1ZZ-C, D2OZ-C	4.000 inches	8.206 inches	"302" in Valley
302 ci	1968–1969	C8AE/ C8OE	D1TE-E, D1ZZ-C, D2OZ-C	4.000 inches	8.206 inches	"302" in Valley
302 ci	1968–1969	C8TE-B	D1TZ-E	4.000 inches	8.206 inches	Truck Block
302 ci	1969	C9TE-C	D1TZ-E	4.000 inches	8.206 inches	—
302 ci	1971–1974	D1OE-AA	D1TZ-E	4.000 inches	8.206 inches (8.229 inches from 1973 to 1976)	—
302 ci	1971–1974	D1TE-AA	D1TZ-E, D1ZZ-C, D2OZ-C	4.000 inches	8.206 inches (8.229 inches from 1973 to 1976)	—
302 ci	1974–1976	D4DE-AA	N/A	4.000 inches	8.229 inches	—
302 ci	1975–1977	D5ZY-AA	N/A	4.000 inches	8.229 inches	—
302 ci	1978–1979	—	D8VE-AA	4.000 inches	8.206 inches	Crank Sensor Provision
302 ci	1980–1982	—	E0AE-DD	4.000 inches	8.206 inches	
302 ci	1982–1984	—	E2AE-KA	4.000 inches	8.206 inches	One-Piece Rear Main Seal
302 ci	1985	—	E5AE-HA	4.000 inches	8.206 inches	Roller Tappet Block
302 ci	1986–1993	—	E6SE-DC	4.000 inches	8.206 inches	Roller Tappet Block, Heavier Webbing
302 ci	1986–95	—	E7TE-PA	4.000 inches	8.206 inches	Roller Tappet, Heavier Webbing
Boss 302	1968–1969	C8FE-B	D1ZZ-B	4.000 inches	8.206 inches	Tunnel Port
Boss 302	1969–1970	D0ZE-A	D1ZZ-B, D1ZZ-C	4.000 inches	8.206 inches	—
Boss 302	1969–1970	D0ZE-B	D1ZZ-B, D1ZZ-C	4.000 inches	8.206 inches	—
Boss 302	1969–1970	D0ZE-C	D1ZZ-B, D1ZZ-C	4.000 inches	8.206 inches	—
Boss 302	1969–1970	D1ZE-B	D1ZZ-B, D1ZZ-C	4.000 inches	8.206 inches	Service Block
351W	1969–1970	C9OE-B	C9OZ-B, D1AZ-E	4.000 inches	9.480 inches	—
351W	1971–1974	D2AE-BA	C9OZ-B, D1AZ-E	4.000 inches	9.480 inches (9.503 inches in 1974)	—
351W	1971–1974	D4AE-AA	C9OZ-B, D1AZ-E	4.000 inches	9.480 inches (9.503 inches in 1974)	—
351W/5.8L	1975–1984	D4AE-DA	C9OZ-B, D1AZ-E	4.000 inches	9.503 inches	—
351W/5.8L	1984–1986	E4AE-FA	—	4.000 inches	9.503 inches	—
351W/5.8L	1985–1986	E5AE-CA	—	4.000 inches	9.503 inches	—
351W/5.8L	1987–1993	E7TE-PA	—	4.000 inches	9.503 inches	Truck Block
351W/5.8L	1989—1993	E9AE-AA	—	4.000 inches	9.503 inches	—
351W/5.8L	1990–1993	F0AE-AA	—	4.000 inches	9.503 inches	—
351W/5.8L	1994–1996	F4TE	—	4.000 inches	9.503 inches	Roller Block

255-ci engine not shown

Buying a Used Block

The purchase of a used engine block requires caution and close attention to detail. How will your engine be used? If your objective is racing, many options are available. As older racers retire, they sell off inventories of used and unused racing castings. Ford Motorsport SVO/ Ford Performance has produced many terrific blocks over the past 30 to 40 years. This means that there are many new and used castings out there. Your best option is new old stock (NOS) if you can find it.

Because we have hit hard economic times in recent years, it is remarkable what you can find tucked away in shops and garages that people are looking to unload. Dreams are forever lost for some who need the cash now. As you shop around, carefully inspect and always measure any block that you consider purchasing. Look for signs of overheating, cracks, discoloration, deck warpage, and shoddy repairs.

It is best to have a used block inspected by a reputable machine shop before having any machine work performed. Few things are more defeating than spending more than $1,000 on machine work only to discover that you have a boat anchor. Have the block cleaned and then check for flaws and damage. A block that has been severely overheated is a block to avoid. A seasoned machinist will be able to determine if what you have is worth saving.

Aftermarket Blocks: Iron or Aluminum?

The aftermarket offers a wealth of blocks for small-block Ford builders. Summit Racing Equipment inventories most of these blocks or can have them drop-shipped to your door from the manufacturer. Summit has Ford Performance, World Products, Speedmaster, Dart, and Bill Mitchell blocks for any project that you may have in mind. There's plenty from which to choose.

The big question among racers is what type of block to use: iron or aluminum? According to Jack McInnis of World Products, cost is a big factor. The cost is reduced by roughly 40 percent or more by selecting iron instead of aluminum.

By "aluminum," I mean cast aluminum, not billet aluminum. Cast and billet aluminum blocks are completely different because billet aluminum requires huge sums of machine time.

Racing enthusiasts tend to focus on the weight difference, which is important, but iron provides a better ring seal because it is more solid, McInnis said. Because iron is more solid than aluminum, it doesn't deflect and distort as much at high cylinder pressures.

If you made a direct comparison

This SVO race block from the 1980s has been prepped with painstaking detail. It is not a roller block yet, but it has been prepped for the lifter spider to become a roller block. This is the G351 block with a 9.200-inch deck height, which isn't a very popular block considering what has come since. Better blocks are available today.

The "WCP" to the right in the valley of this SVO block stands for Windsor Casting Plant. Earlier blocks would have been "WF" for Windsor Foundry.

between engines with iron and aluminum blocks and had all other variables be the same, the iron-block engine would produce a bit more horsepower than the equivalent aluminum block, McInnis said.

Aluminum blocks are strong today compared to those that were available in the past, but a properly built iron block is still ultimately stronger. If you happen to experience a catastrophic engine failure, an iron block is typically going to hold up better.

The rigidity and higher tensile strength of iron makes it inherently better at handling large amounts of power and huge amounts of boost when compared to aluminum. Plenty of racers make lots of power with aluminum blocks. Where the rubber meets the road, tuning is everything to engine survival. However, aluminum is less tolerant to the extremes when compared to iron.

With a lot of boost or nitrous oxide, the block casting can twist and move to the point of destruction. This can subsequently lead to other components failing because they don't have the support that is required at that moment, McInnis said.

Generally, an iron block allows components to live longer and provides better reliability as a result. While there are classes across several different racing disciplines where iron blocks are required by the rules, there are also situations where iron is simply a better option for a given application. In classes where the cars are heavy anyway or marine applications where weight is not a big consideration, what you lose in additional weight can be compensated for with additional power.

Ford Performance

Ford Performance offers a great playing field when it comes to high-performance blocks for small-block Ford projects. Everything from a modest 5.0L roller street block to an all-out race block is available. The most significant block introduced by Ford Performance is the Boss 302 block: M-6010-BOSS302. The M-6010-BOSS302 was a long time coming. It was the replacement for the 302 M-6010-A50 Sportsman block, which was in production for many years. In fact, if you can find a good A50 block, it's a good pick for a small-block project.

The M-6010-BOSS302 block is cast from the latest high-tech casting techniques at Ford's Cleveland foundry. Refining this technique came from years of practice developing durable NASCAR blocks that have a fierce reputation for reliability.

What makes today different than the 1970s is CAD (computer-aided design), which is used in the casting modeling. Once Ford adds virtual machining to the casting model, it's time to calculate how much molten metal needs to be poured into the sand casting. Although this process saves Ford money, it also means less weight. Cylinders are siamesed to make the block stronger. Although the new Ford Racing Boss 302 block had some teething problems early on, it has panned out to be one of the best aftermarket blocks that Ford has ever produced.

The classic Ford Racing Sportsman block is an excellent value if you can find one. The disappointing part was the halt in production years ago of these A50 Sportsman blocks, which were such an excellent value for the money at around $1,000.

If you're building a warmed-up street engine, the discontinued 1985–1999 5.0L production roller block has been a great disappointment because Ford gave the option of starting with a new stock block instead of searching all over for a standard-bore used block. These blocks were plentiful and cheap. Summit Racing Equipment had a huge inventory of them, as did Ford until supplies dried up.

The M-6010-A50 Sportsman block is a great value because plenty of them are still out there—both used and NOS. Tipping the scales at 135 pounds, the Sportsman block offers nodular-iron architecture with wide two-bolt main caps. These blocks can be stroked to 347 ci. The A50 Sportsman block is a great direct replacement for the standard-production, bread-and-butter 1985–1999 5.0L roller block.

Although Ford Performance offers more race blocks than it does street blocks, it makes decision making easy when building a street machine or a weekend racer. The M-6010-BOSS302 is a great street/strip block, but it's a bit cost prohibitive for those on a tight budget. The A50 Sportsman block is more practical in terms of cost, but it is no longer available from Ford Performance.

Your mission and budget will determine which block you select. Without any doubt, the A50 Sportsman is a more practical block for the street and strip. You can throw 450 hp at this block without spending a fortune.

Ford Performance Blocks (Not all listed are still available from Ford Performance)

M-6010-BOSS302 (302 Based)

Use	Professional Competition or Street
Block Material	Cast Iron
Nominal Deck Height	8.206 inches
Displacement	363 ci
Cylinder Design	Siamese
Cylinder Bore Diameter Range	4.000 to 4.125 inches
Oil Sump Design	Wet Sump
Crankshaft Main Journal Diameter	2.2480 inches
Main Cap Bolts	Four-Bolt on Main Number-2, -3, and -4
Main Cap Material	Nodular Iron
Maximum Stroke	3.400 inches
Rear Main Seal Type	One Piece
Cam Bearing Design	M-6261-R351 Common Journal or M-6261-J351 for Standard Camshaft

M-6010-C451 (351W Based)

Use	Professional Competition
Block Material	Cast Aluminum
Nominal Deck Height	9.200 inches
Displacement	427 ci
Cylinder Design	Siamese
Cylinder Bore Diameter Range	4.000 to 4.125 inches
Oil Sump Design	Dry Sump (Requires external oil pump/filter system)
Crankshaft Main Journal Diameter	2.750 inches
Main Cap Bolts	Four-Bolt Main Caps
Main Cap Material	Billet Steel
Maximum Stroke	4.000 inches
Rear Main Seal Type	One Piece
Cam Bearing Design	M-6261-C450 Common Journal (not compatible with hydraulic-roller camshaft)

M-6010-C58 (351W Based)

Use	Amateur Competition
Block Material	Cast Iron
Nominal Deck Height	9.500 inches
Displacement	408 ci
Cylinder Design	Siamese
Cylinder Bore Diameter Range	4.000 to 4.030 inches
Oil Sump Design	Wet Sump
Crankshaft Main Journal Diameter	3.000 inches
Main Cap Bolts	Two-Bolt Main Caps
Main Cap Material	Nodular Iron
Maximum Stroke	4.000 inches
Rear Main Seal Type	One Piece
Cam Bearing Design	M-6261-R351 Common Journal or M-6261-J351 for Standard Camshaft

M-6010-G351 and N351 (351W Based)

Use	Professional Competition Only
Block Material	Cast Iron
Nominal Deck Height	9.200 inches (G351), 9.500 inches (N351)
Displacement	434 ci
Cylinder Design	Not Siamese
Cylinder Bore Diameter Range	4.000 to 4.030 inches
Oil Sump Design	Wet Sump
Crankshaft Main Journal Diameter	2.749 inches
Main Cap Bolts	Four-Bolt on Main Number-2, -3, and -4
Main Cap Material	Nodular Iron
Maximum Stroke	4.250 inches
Rear Main Seal Type	One Piece
Cam Bearing Design	Standard Type

M-6010-R452 (351W Based)

Use	Professional Competition
Block Material	Cast Iron
Nominal Deck Height	9.200 inches
Displacement Capacity	427 ci
Cylinder Design	Siamese
Cylinder Bore Diameter Range	4.000 to 4.180 inches
Oil Sump Design	Dry Sump (Requires external oil pump/filter system)
Crankshaft Main Journal Diameter	2.248 inches
Main Cap Bolts	Four-Bolt Main Caps
Main Cap Material	Nodular Iron
Maximum Stroke	4.000 inches
Rear Main Seal Type	One Piece
Cam Bearing Design	M-6261-R351 Common Journal or M-6261-J351 for Standard Camshaft

M-6010-V351 (351W Based)

Use	Professional Competition
Block Material	Cast Iron Block
Nominal Deck Height	9.200 inches
Displacement Capacity	427 ci
Cylinder Design	Siamese
Cylinder Bore Diameter Range	4.000 to 4.125 inches
Oil Sump Design	Wet Sump
Crankshaft Main Journal Diameter	2.249 inches
Main Cap Bolts	Four-Bolt on Main Number-2, -3, and -4
Main Cap Material	Nodular Iron
Maximum Stroke	3.400 inches
Rear Main Seal Type	One Piece
Cam Bearing Design	M-6261-R351 Common Journal or M-6261-J351 for Standard Camshaft

M-6010-W351 (351W Based)	
Use	Professional Competition
Block Material	Cast Iron
Nominal Deck Height	9.500 inches
Displacement Capacity	454 ci
Cylinder Design	Siamese
Cylinder Bore Diameter Range	4.000 to 4.125 inches
Oil Sump Design	Wet Sump
Crankshaft Main Journal Diameter	2.2480 inches
Main Cap Bolts	Four-Bolt on Main Number-2, -3, -4, and -5
Main Cap Material	Nodular Iron
Maximum Stroke	4.250 inches
Rear Main Seal Type	One Piece
Cam Bearing Design	M-6261-R351 Common Journal or M-6261-J351 for Standard Camshaft

Dart Machinery

Dart Machinery offers a broad selection of Ford blocks. The Dart Special High Performance (SHP) Ford block is engineered to popular performance and racing applications with an 8.200-inch (302 ci), 9.200-inch (351C), or 9.500-inch (351W) deck height and a choice of 4.000-inch or 4.125-inch siamesed cylinder bores that can safely be bored to 4.185 inches. Brute steel main caps are splayed four-bolt on the center three and two-bolt on number-1 and number-5, and utilize 1/2-inch bolts. The lifter valley is machined to accept the factory roller-lifter guides and retainer.

The Dart's priority main oiling system directs oil to the main bearings first for more confident lubrication. There's no provision for oil restrictors. You get extended cylinder bores for improved piston support at the bottom end, extra-thick decks to ensure a solid head-gasket seal, blind head-bolt holes (which means that these don't go into the water jackets), and steel four-bolt main caps on number-2, number-3, and number-4 with splayed outer support bolts. These blocks use most stock components and accessories. In addition, scalloped water jackets increase coolant flow around the cylinder bores to prevent detonation, which extends engine life and produces consistent cylinder temperatures. These castings are among the best in the industry.

Dart's Iron Eagle blocks, like the SHP, are designed to work with stock components. Designed from the ground up for hard-core racing, the Iron Eagle addresses all the weaknesses of the factory castings. The Iron Eagle block is cast from premium high-strength iron with extra-thick cylinder walls and decks. In addition, the main webs are beefier and fitted with steel four-bolt main caps.

The Iron Eagle block has siamesed cylinders. The standard 4.000-inch and 4.125-inch cylinder bores can be safely bored to 4.185 inches in diameter. These extended cylinder bores offer improved piston support.

Four deck heights are available: 8.200 inches (302), 8.700 inches (stroker 302), 9.200 inches (351C), and 9.500 inches (351W). These allow for increased displacements up to 468 ci. Down under, steel four-bolt main-bearing caps are standard. Three center caps offer splayed outer bolts for maximum strength. Two main-bearing diameters are available: 302 (2.249 inches) or 351C (2.749 inches) with a small- or large-journal crankshaft.

The Iron Eagle upgraded oiling system has been completely redesigned with a low-restriction, priority-main oiling system with a rear external oil-pump feed. Reinforced cylinder-head-bolt bosses are blind tapped (instead of into the water jackets) to prevent leaks and produce accurate torque readings. Extra-thick decks prevent head-gasket leaks.

If you want something better, the Iron Eagle Pro block offers upgraded main bolts to main studs, reduced 0.250-inch main oil feed holes, a reduced 0.090-inch cam-to-crank oil feed (for Babbit cam use), a removed cam-to-crank oil feed (for roller cam use), a removed oil filter location, a removed front -10AN oil feed, a removed rear lifter crossover, an external dry sump or external wet sump only, and a removed stock oil-pump-mounting boss. If you'd like more, you can get it machined for threaded freeze plugs, a removed distributor bore for

Invest in an aftermarket block from Dart, Bill Mitchell, World Products, or Ford Performance when the power rises above 500 hp. Shop carefully and read the details before purchasing.

coil-on-plug applications, and a tie bar or keyed lifter bushings.

Dart also offers aluminum race blocks with pressed-in dry sleeves, upgraded oiling, and steel four-bolt main caps. These blocks are cast from RMR cast aluminum alloy (Dart's proprietary alloy) for superior strength. As with the iron blocks, these castings offer extended cylinder bores to improve piston support. Four deck heights are available: 8.200 inches (302), 8.700 inches (stroker 302), 9.200 inches (351C), and 9.500 inches (351W). These allow displacements up to 450 ci.

Siamesed cylinders with either standard 4.000-inch or 4.125-inch cylinders can be safely bored to 4.165 inches in diameter. Ductile iron sleeves and thicker walls prevent cracking and provide an excellent ring seal. Steel four-bolt main-bearing caps are standard. Three center caps have splayed outer bolts for maximum strength. The rear main cap uses the standard late-model, one-piece seal.

As with all Dart blocks, the upgraded oiling system has been completely redesigned with a low-restriction priority-main oiling system that has a rear external oil-pump feed. Dual crossovers allow oil flow to be metered with restrictors for roller lifter cams and/or roller rocker arms to reduce oil flow and windage. Reinforced head-bolt bosses are blind tapped to prevent leaks and produce accurate torque readings. Extra-thick decks prevent head gasket leaks.

Speedmaster

Speedmaster was founded in 1979 as Pete's Performance down under in Australia, which was a traditional speed shop with modest beginnings. It grew aggressively from there. Speedmaster began as a machine shop and engine builder. This passionate company has grown into a worldwide high-performance source for engines and parts. Today, Speedmaster has distribution centers and offices in Sydney, Australia; Los Angeles, California; and Shanghai, China.

You can expect a nice variety of Speedmaster 351W blocks from Summit Racing Equipment. These PCE castings are world-class. This 351W block is optimal for the street racer and all-out racer alike with added strength and the great potential for displacement. It was designed to handle up to 1,500 hp. Each block is cast from high-quality, high-density iron with thicker cylinder walls and decks. The block's webs are thicker and are fitted with billet steel four-bolt-main caps. This is one example of what you can get for roughly $2,500.

BMP

Bill Mitchell Hard Core Racing Products (BMP) has been around since the 1980s with a range of products from radiators to race engines. Later, Bill Mitchell founded World Products, a manufacturer of cast-iron and aluminum engine blocks and heads.

In 2011, Bill Mitchell Jr. assumed full control of BMP and elected to take this brand to the next level, acquiring the entire aluminum product line of World Products. This line includes engine blocks, cylinder heads, and intake manifolds. These

World Products produced the first aftermarket Ford blocks and continues moving forward with terrific "Man O'War" iron blocks that can handle more than 1,000 hp. World Products blocks are available from Bill Mitchell Products (BMP) and Summit Racing Equipment.

BMP offers a variety of aluminum (shown) and iron blocks. BMP has its own brand of aluminum blocks along with iron blocks from World Products. Selecting either iron or aluminum depends on the type of racing that you intend to do.

racing products are now marketed and sold under the BMP brand name. To do this, BMP decided to change foundries and move to modern, state-of-the-art facilities.

BMP made upgrades to the tooling to add features. It also moved to new, more-capable machining centers. BMP built entirely new machine fixtures to guarantee the absolute

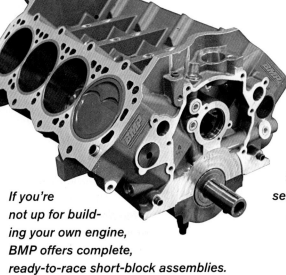

The Ford Performance Boss 302 block has been around long enough that it has been proven around the world—both on the track and on the street. It replaced the classic Sportsman block that was so popular in the 1990s. By preserving many of the dimensions and features from the original 289/302/351W blocks, the Boss block is a compatible replacement.

If you're not up for building your own engine, BMP offers complete, ready-to-race short-block assemblies. Contact BMP for details.

highest standard of appearance and precision for its products.

If you were a performance enthusiast looking for cylinder heads back in the day, your choices were limited to scrounging through salvage yards, going to the dealership for OEM parts, or spending a small fortune on aftermarket aluminum racing heads. There was no in-between option. Bill Mitchell took a long look at that. Bill and his skilled team of engineering and manufacturing personnel collaborated to develop an affordable cast-iron head, beginning with Chevrolet and growing into Ford and Chrysler applications (heads and later blocks). BMP offers a variety of Ford blocks for your project.

World Products Iron Blocks from BMP

World Products needs no introduction with Ford enthusiasts, and you can get its products from BMP. This company has been producing high-performance Ford blocks and heads for at least three decades. The engineering team at World Products has worked with leading Ford racers and professional engine builders through the years to develop the "Man O'War" family of replacement iron blocks for the 302 and 351W

Ford small-block engines. These blocks are available in three deck heights to ensure compatibility with all popular Ford OEM and aftermarket cylinder head/intake manifold combinations.

The World Products Man O'War Ford blocks have been created utilizing contemporary computer-aided-design (CAD) and computer-aided-manufacturing (CAM) technology to achieve more precisely detailed blocks than ever before possible through conventional foundry methods. In addition, they're made to QS-9000-quality standards, which are the highest in the industry.

World Products upgraded the iron blocks to a 40,000-psi iron alloy and added material to the main webs for incredible strength. The first main web is 0.080 inch thicker. The center three main webs have been increased by 0.030 inch. Main-cap bolts have grown from 7/16-inch to 1/2-inch ARP fasteners, which leaves more material in the main webs to

The Boss 351 block from Ford Performance is a proven casting that is on a par with the short-deck Boss 302 and has all of the same benefits. It will drop right in place of a stock 351W or 351C block.

The Ford Performance 427 short-block allows you to build your way by using your choice of heads, cam, intake, and oil pan. This is the perfect foundation to build a powerful 9.500-inch-deck, 351W–based engine. Ford Performance said that this is the same short-block that was used with the 575-hp Z427 crate engine. You get a forged steel crankshaft, brute I-beam connecting rods with floating piston pins, and the race-ready Boss 351 block.

strengthen the main web structure further.

The Man O'War blocks come in various deck heights to match the application. The 8.200-inch block (302) is a direct bolt-in for 5.0L Mustangs and is compatible with OEM heads and exhaust systems. World Products also offers 9.200- and 9.500-inch-deck blocks (351W). The Man O'War block was designed completely from scratch (in collaboration with a leading NASCAR team) using CAD, CAM, and 3-D design technology.

Budget Blocks

The aftermarket is crawling with reconditioned 289/302/351W blocks that are ready for final detail work and assembly. For less than $1,000 you can get a reconditioned and fully machined block from Competition Products, which is just one example of what's available. Check all dimensions via your local machine shop and make sure that the pistons are matched to the bores.

Competition Products begins with select Ford cores and puts them through an extensive cleaning and machining process. They are chemically cleaned and Magnafluxed for cracks. Then, they are bored and honed on Sunnen equipment. The decks are milled and checked. Then, the blocks get final prep, including freeze plugs and Dura-Bond cam bearings.

These reconditioned blocks are sold as performance blocks, and, therefore, no warranty is expressed or implied. If you get a flawed block, you're stuck with it. This means that you must thoroughly examine your block when it arrives. This goes for any used or reconditioned block

that you may purchase. Confirm the block's condition the minute that it arrives. You don't want to find out months or years later that you have a flawed block. Do not wait. Have a trusted machine shop inspect and confirm its condition before you begin assembly.

Block Preparation

You want a block with perfectly machined surfaces that will mate well and seal tight without conflict. This calls for extreme measures in machining and painstaking attention to detail. This is why you must enlist an experienced and trusted machine shop. Before spending a lot of money on a block, it must first be cleaned and inspected. Then, it must be confirmed to be fit for service. This is a good investment, especially if you discover you have a bad block.

Machine shops will not clean and machine a block and then refund your money because it is cracked, was bored oversize beyond salvage, was windowed by a stray connecting rod and repaired, or suffers from

some other type of defect.

First, determine if you have a usable block. Begin with a pressure test to confirm its integrity. Then, do a complete thermal cleaning, including the removal of all freeze plugs (also known as Welsh plugs) and oil gallery plugs followed by a visual and magnetic particle inspection. This is an investment that you will have to make in a block casting before spending the real money on machine work.

Go into water jackets with a high-powered magnet to catch slag and other metal debris that can cause cooling-system troubles. I've seen freeze plugs that have been knocked inside the water jackets by careless rebuilders and factory autoworkers. Do this even with a new block. Measure the cylinder-bore size from top to bottom and sonic check the cylinder walls and block decks. Perform a pressure test. Line bore should also be checked. Check the cam-bore-to-line-bore centerlines. Check the cam journals for any irregularities. Examine the lifter bores.

Block cleaning should be an ongoing process throughout the

Block prep is everything to a successful engine build even if you're building a warmed-up stocker. MCE Engines in Los Angeles, California, often stresses the importance of the details with an examination of block integrity and GE Glyptal 1201 coating in the valley and other drainback areas to improve return flow. Screens at the drain holes keep unwanted debris out of the oil pan and pump.

MCE Engines always drilled a small 0.020-inch oil hole in this oil-gallery plug to improve timing-chain lubrication. Return oil isn't always enough to keep the chain and sprocket adequately lubricated at high RPM.

Lifter bores should always be honed for improved oil control and stability.

machining phases. Have the machinist clean the block after each machining phase to ensure that debris doesn't accumulate in oil galleries, water jackets, and other cavities.

Machine work includes cylinder boring and honing if bores are tapered beyond 0.0010 inch. The maximum wear limit is 0.010 inch over before you must go to the next oversize. Where possible, bore and hone to 0.020-inch oversize instead of 0.030 inch, which buys you more block life. If wear is minimal and boring is unnecessary, you must at least do a fine finish hone and ridge removal. The purpose of boring is not only to take cylinders to the next oversize but also to match each piston to a hone-matched bore.

Make sure that your machine shop uses a torque plate for honing, which simulates cylinder-head installation and gets the bore as it will be once heads are installed and torqued down. Three different stones are typically used in the honing process. They become progressively finer as the process goes until the machinist achieves a fine crosshatch pattern.

Main saddles need to be align honed until they are true. Align honing puts a nice crosshatch pattern in the bearing saddles, which provides good bearing crush and security. Main saddles require boring when they are worn beyond their limits, which involves milling main-cap mating surfaces and then boring and honing the installed caps. This is on a par with reconditioning connecting rods. One thing that machine shops rarely do is cam bore align honing. However, for good cam bearing security, ask the machine shop to check and hone yours if necessary. It's worth the expense to get a good crosshatch pattern.

Decks should be measured across and corner to corner and then milled the most minimal amount that is necessary. Block-deck warpage any greater than 0.003 inch across 6 inches or more calls for deck milling. Deck height is the distance from the crankshaft centerline to the top of each deck. Once the decks are milled, your machine shop should put a taper at the top of each bore to ease piston/ring installation.

Once the block is in paint, spray the cylinder walls and interior surfaces with WD-40 for corrosion prevention. You don't want rusty cylinder walls and bearing saddles. In a damp climate, it doesn't take long for them to get that way.

Some block cracking can be repaired via welding or J-B Weld. J-B Weld is a two-part catalyzed product that works well with cracked cast iron. If it is properly mixed and given the necessary time to cure, it will last the life of any engine block. For J-B Weld to work effectively, you need a clean surface and a crack that has been carefully stop drilled at each end. Just a small 1/16-inch stop drill hole at each end slows and stops cracking. Then weld or use J-B Weld in the crack. I don't suggest the use of J-B Weld at the cylinder walls and decks where stresses can be extreme. Your machine shop will know best for what call to make regarding repair. Some blocks are cracked beyond repair.

Ford Small Block Specifications

Engine	Cylinder Bore Diameter	Main Bearing Journal Runout	Main Bearing Bore	Lifter Bore Diameter	Distributor Shaft Bore Diameter	Head Gasket Surface
221ci	3.500 inches	0.002–0.003 inch	2.4412–2.4420 inches	0.8752–0.8767 inch	0.4525–0.4541 inch	0.003 inch in any 6 inches or 0.007 inch overall
260 ci	3.803–3.8027 inches	0.002–0.003 inch	2.4412–2.4420 inches	0.8752–0.8767 inch	0.4525–0.4541 inch	0.003 inch in any 6 inches or 0.007 inch overall
289 ci	4.000–4.0024 inches	0.002–0.003 inch	2.4412–2.4420 inches	0.8752–0.8767 inch	0.4525–0.4541 inch	0.003 inch in any 6 inches or 0.007 inch overall
302 ci	4.000–4.0024 inches	0.002–0.003 inch	2.4412–2.4420 inches	0.8752–0.8767 inch	0.4525–0.4541 inch	0.003 inch in any 6 inches or 0.007 inch overall
351W	4.000–4.0024 inches	0.004 inch	3.1922–3.1930 inches	0.8752–0.8767 inch	0.5155–0.5171 inch	0.003 inch in any 6 inches or 0.007 inch overall

Oil and cooling passages should be chamfered (as shown) to reduce fluid turbulence.

I enjoy seeing a clean finish hone with a good crosshatch pattern that is void of scratches for proper ring seating during break-in.

Fasteners and Clean Threads

Block preparation includes thread chasing to ensure proper fastener torque readings. Lubricate every bolt hole with WD-40 and chase it with a thread chaser until the fasteners roll smoothly. Tap damaged threads or repair them with a Heli-Coil insert. Once the threads are clear, blast them with a soapy solution and compressed air. Then, spray WD-40 in the hole to prevent corrosion.

When it comes to fasteners, I suggest the use of ARP fasteners throughout because there is no better fastener available. You will learn that some ARP kits don't have all of the correct fasteners you're going to need, which means that you will need to do it piecemeal for your small-block build.

I suggest using main studs even if you're building a stocker for greater bottom-end security. Main studs provide greater security due to the way that they are seated in the block. Main studs offer greater structural integrity, which prevents main-cap movement. Head studs make cylinder-head removal difficult if you have to remove them in the car. However, if

you're going to push the limits of a small-block Ford (such as using nitrous oxide, supercharging, or using high RPM/high compression for extended periods), studs are the better choice.

Never torque fasteners without lubrication and always torque them in one-third torque values. Then, recheck torque. So, if you have a full torque value of 80 ft-lbs, the first phase should be to 26.6 ft-lbs, the second phase should be to 53.3 ft-lbs, and the final phase should be to 80 ft-lbs. Then, check total torque. No one torques fasteners to 26.6 or 53.3 ft-lbs. You may round it off to the nearest tenth.

Why is bolt torque so important? Tightening a fastener is about clamping force between two or more components and having them stay together. As you tighten a fastener, you are working against threads in the process of pulling two or more components together. You're also contributing to bolt stretch and tension.

As torque is applied, bolt threads draw the threaded face and bolt head closer together, which stretches the fastener and applies tension. Bolt tension works by loading the bolt head, which provides stretch before the

It is important to remove the rope seal retaining pin from the number-5 main cap before installing a new rear main seal. The original rear main seals were little more than some rope with a pin inserted in the cap to secure the rope seal. However, replacement rubber/silicone lip seals will distort if you leave this pin installed.

nut is secure and tight. The tensioner is clamped to the bolt's threads and pushes against the flange in the surface being bolted. This provides a very consistent amount of bolt stretch, which ensures uniform bolt stretch and a uniform clamping force on the components. This is why you must invest in a torque wrench and other appropriate tools. Do not tighten fasteners based on feel.

ROTATING ASSEMBLY

The 289/302/351W nodular-iron crankshaft is a durable crank due to main journal sizing and the consistency of improved nodular iron. You may also infuse power with an affordable aftermarket stroker kit. If you stud the mains and beef up the rods with ARP fasteners, you're ahead of the game. The 1M/2M/3M factory crank is a piece that can withstand up to 6,500 rpm. If you work out the stress risers and imperfections along with nitriding, you will have a crank that can take a beating.

Because there are many torsional stresses on a crankshaft, a lot of thought needs to be given to crankshaft selection. Although the hot ticket always seems to be steel crankshafts, they're truly unnecessary for a street/strip build. Cast is good for anything up to 500 hp. If you're going to push it beyond 500 hp, use steel. If you're using nitrous oxide or a blower, use steel to get durability.

Crank twist and oscillation affect timing and power output. As pistons and rods rise to the compression/ignition stroke, oscillation becomes more intense, acting on not only the crankshaft but also the connecting rods and pistons. It all moves violently with changes in power

The 221/260/289/302 bottom end looks like this with tapered main caps and either a "1M" (2.870-inch stroke) or "2M" (3.000-inch stroke) cast crank. When properly prepared, these cranks can withstand 450 to 500 hp.

application. The crank's torsional behavior rebounds against the piston and rod as they ascend on the compression stroke. There's also the harmonic damper, which acts as a shock absorber for crank twist. As the crank rebounds, it works on the balancer, which softens rebound shock and reduces the risk of crankshaft breakage. Regardless of how you look at this dynamic, cyclic fatigue issues affect crankshaft life.

How do you recondition a crankshaft to make the most of its durability? Automakers engineer tremendous strength into even the most modest cast-iron crankshafts.

The fillet radius is the most common failure point between journals and the rest of the crank. A mid-journal failure or a break at a counterweight is rare. Pay close attention to the fillet area with proper machining and finishing technique, plus the bearing's relationship with the fillet. Radiuses must be identical.

Machine the crank journals to the bearings and swap bearings around to get the optimal clearances. Micropolish the journals and fillet radiuses to get the best oil wedge for the best results. Main and rod journals get extremely hot, especially under a load at high RPM, where oil

Whether you're building a stocker or a weekend warrior, stud the main caps with ARP studs to provide rigidity.

Small-block Ford crankshaft identification is easy. Look for a marking, such as this "1M," in the first counterweight, which indicates a 2.870-inch stroke (221/260/289). A "2M" indicates a 3.000-inch stroke (302). Later 5.0L cranks are stamped "2MA." The 351W has a "3M" marking that indicates a 3.500-inch stroke.

Aside from the wider main caps (not shown), the 289 High Performance rods (identifiable by orange paint) have 3/8-inch bolts, cast pistons with ductile iron rings, and a standard "1M" cast crank that has been handpicked and Brinell tested for hardness. This is indicated by a dimple or punch mark in the first crankshaft journal (also look for orange paint).

This is an original 289 High Performance bottom end. The crank and rod both have orange paint dabs for quick identification during manufacturing.

temperatures can briefly be around 350°F to 400°F, which can cook the oil, rendering it useless.

Conventional engine oil begins to break down at 260°F. Synthetic oil begins to breakdown at 300°F. Oil can tolerate extremely high temperatures for a short amount of time, which is why steady volume across the bearings and journals is important.

If the machining process and mock-up show excessive crankshaft endplay, King Engine Bearing has two affordable options: MaxFlange and ProFlange thrust bearings. Max-Flange is a process used on all King engine bearings. It reduces crankshaft

This is a 351W crank (3.500-inch stroke) from the 1980s with a casting number of "E4AE-BA," which was designed for one-piece rear main seal blocks. This means that it is a "7M" crank. Prior to the 1980s, the 351W crank was considered to be a "3M" crank with the same 3.500-inch stroke.

If you use a dual-roller timing set, do not use this stock oil slinger. It will interfere with the chain, which can do serious engine damage.

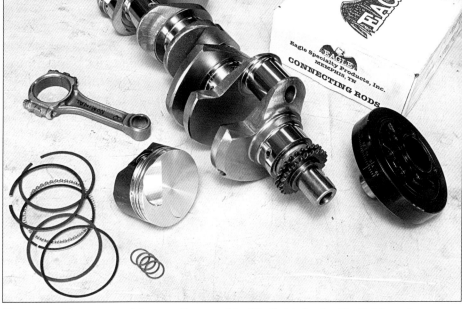

If you want brute street torque for good traffic light–to–traffic light performance, use a cast-steel stroker crank, heavy-duty I-beam rods, and either forged or hypereutectic pistons. Take your 289/302 engine to 331 or 347 ci to increase torque dramatically. A 351W can be stroked to 427 ci for big-block performance.

Crankshaft

The 221, 260, and 289 engines all employ the same "1M" cast-iron crankshaft with a 2.870-inch stroke and 2.249-inch main journals. The "1M" crank isn't as widely available as it used to be because it has been decades since Ford produced this crankshaft, and good cores are hard to find.

The 289 High Performance V-8 had the same "1M" cast crank that was found in the 221, 260, and 289 engines, with one exception: a Brinell-hardness-test dimple to confirm integrity. This didn't make a 289 High Performance crankshaft a better piece. Instead, it identifies the 289 High Performance crankshaft as a hand-picked part with verified integrity.

endplay by supplying a flange on the high side of the tolerance to compensate for excessive crankshaft thrust wear. ProFlange offers a line of bearing sets with oversized flanges, which allows the crank's thrust to be ground to 0.010-, 0.020-, or 0.030-inch undersized. Both approaches are designed to save crankshafts from rework or replacement.

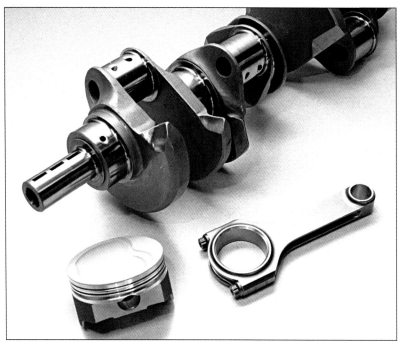

Oil control and flow should be improved even with a stock build. Journal oil holes should be chamfered (and polished) to allow volume across the bearings and journals. This should be performed by a qualified machine shop.

This is an extreme setup: a steel crank with knife-edged counterweights for reduced windage and drag. H-beam rods and forged pistons can withstand well beyond 1,000 hp. It's important to know where your components come from. Use a proven source, such as Scat Enterprises, which does its manufacturing in house.

Another difference is the Hi-Po's slide-on steel plate counterweight used to offset the additional weight created by larger 3/8-inch rod bolts.

When you're shopping for a crankshaft, be sure that you're not looking at a bogus Hi-Po crank with a bogus Brinell test mark and orange paint. These cranks are out there, waiting for unsuspecting buyers. A Brinell-tested "1M" crankshaft isn't required because Magnafluxing and hardness testing are available via reputable machine shops.

The 302 cast crankshaft with a 3.000-inch stroke and 2.249-inch main journals is identified by a "2M" on the first counterweight/journal. It is not interchangeable with 221, 260, or 289 rods unless you're planning to use a custom piston because it employs a slightly shorter 5.090-inch connecting rod.

Later, Ford made changes to the 2M crankshaft to improve fuel economy via weight reduction. Crankshaft production shifted from Ford's North American foundries around Detroit, which were shut down, to those in Canada. Be mindful of these changes when you're shopping for a 302 crankshaft. The most rugged 2M 302 crankshaft you can get is what Ford used in 5.0L High Output V-8s from 1982–2000. It can be identified by "2MA" or "2ME" markings. It is clearly a different crank than earlier 2M castings. It is also machined for a one-piece rear main seal, which means that it tends to leak with a two-piece-seal block.

When 302/5.0L crankshaft manufacturing shifted to Canada, these cranks became stronger, which is one reason why the 5.0L High Output engine is rugged and depend-able. In your search for a good 5.0L 2MA or 2ME crankshaft, don't mistakenly pick up one for the 255-ci (4.2L) engine, which looks the same externally with the same 3.000-inch stroke but has hollow rod journals for reduced weight, which also compromises strength.

The 1969–1970 Boss 302 has the same 4.000-inch bore and 3.000-inch stroke as a standard 302, except it has a Boss 302-specific forged-steel crankshaft that is marked "D0ZE-A" or "7FE-8."

The 351 Windsor's nodular-iron crankshaft has a 3.500-inch stroke with 3.000-inch main journals and a "3M" on the first counterweight/journal. A forged-steel crankshaft was never available from the factory for the 351W. The 351W's 3M cranks are extremely durable and can take a lot of punishment (given ample oil supply). When the 351W engine was upgraded to a one-piece rear main seal in 1985, its revised nodular-iron crankshaft received a revised "7MA" identification code.

Crankshaft Identification

Displacement	Year	Casting/Part Number	Stroke	Other Information
221 ci	1962–1963	C2OZ, C3OZ "1M"	2.870 inches	Cast iron, first year (1962) no markings
260 ci	1962–1964	C2OZ, C3OZ "1M"	2.870 inches	Cast iron, first year (1962) no markings
289 ci	1963–1968	C3OZ "1M"	2.870 inches	Cast iron
289 ci High Performance	1963–1967	C3OZ "1M"	2.870 inches	Cast iron, Brinell hardness test mark on journal, orange/yellow paint markings on counterweights
302 ci	1968–1981	C8AZ-A, "2M"	3.000 inches	Cast iron
302 ci	1978–1982	E0SE-AD	3.000 inches	Cast iron, special crankshaft for Lincoln Versailles (crank trigger) with EEC-I system.
302 ci/5.0L	1979–2000	D9TE-EA, E1AE-AA, E2AE-EA, "2MA," "2ME"	3.000 inches	Cast iron, all 5.0L crankshafts and blocks from December 1, 1982–up have a one-piece rear main seal with no crank seal lip. Watch out for this change. 50-ounce offset balance.
255 ci/4.2L	1980–1982	D9TE-EA, E1AE-AA, E2AE-EA, "2MA," "2ME"	3.000 inches	Cast iron, all 5.0L crankshafts and blocks from December 1, 1982–up have a one-piece rear main seal with no crank seal lip. Watch out for this change. 50-ounce offset balance.
Boss 302	1969–1970	D0ZE-A or 7FE-8	3.000 inches	Forged steel
351W	1969–1972	"3M" C9OZ-A	3.500 inches	Cast iron
351W	1973–1979	"3MA" C9OZ-A	3.500 inches	Cast iron
351W	1980–1984	"3C"	3.500 inches	Cast iron
351W/5.8L	1985–1996	"7M" "7MA"	3.500 inches	Cast iron, one-piece rear main seal

Crankshaft Selection

A cast crank generally has a rough surface with narrow parting lines. A forged-steel crank has smoother surfaces and wide parting lines due to the forging process. Steel billet, which is very expensive, is in a class of its own: racing.

If you take a small hammer and tap a forged crank, it will ring like a bell with a long resonance afterward. A cast-iron crank rings but not with the clarity and crispness of a forged crank. If you have a cracked crank, it won't ring at all, and there typically will be a buzzy resonance.

Crankshaft materials vary considerably and there are plenty from which to choose: steel billet on the high end, forged steel, malleable steel, and nodular iron (cast iron/cast steel). On stroker-kit websites you will see the words, "cast steel," which is marketing language for cast iron or nodular iron. It sounds more upscale than cast iron, but it is little more than nodular iron.

What are the differences between nodular and cast iron? There are different grades of what is essentially cast iron. The grade depends on the alloy and quenching (heat treating). Crankshafts and camshafts, to name two examples, are ductile or nodular iron (ASTM A339) at 310 on the Brinell hardness scale. Iron with low carbon content is known as steel.

Nodular iron is also known as ductile iron. The separation of graphite in nodular form is like the separation of graphite in gray cast iron, except that the additives that are included in the mix facilitate the graphite to take nodular shape. Hence, the term "nodular" is used. Ductile iron continues to find wide uses in the automotive industry. The graphite structure in the iron is a primary reason for the higher strength and ductility. Ductile irons are used in the production of crankshafts, gears, rocker arms, and even disc-brake calipers.

Crank preparation includes Magnafluxing (an electromagnetic process of checking for cracks), grinding and polishing, radiusing the journals, and removing all of the stress risers. Removing stress risers is crack prevention. Cross-drill where possible and chamfer the oil holes to improve oil flow at the journals. Chamfering improves the oil flow to the bearings and journals by reducing fluid turbulence. In other words, a broader oil-hole surface area at the journal increases volume.

Scat, Eagle, Ford Performance, Coast High Performance, Summit Racing Equipment, Speedmaster, and other sources sell stroker kits. It is important to know what you're paying for when you're shopping for engine kits.

Forged Steel

Cast, nodular iron, and cast-steel crankshafts are the cheapest and most common because they're easy to manufacture. Molten liquid iron is poured into a sand cast mold, cooled, heat treated, and machined to what looks like a crankshaft. Forged-steel crankshafts, on the other hand, require a more involved process because there are more manufacturing steps. A nearly molten steel alloy ingot is heated to approximately 2,200 to 2,600°F and rammed into the shape of a crankshaft in a die in excess of 240,000 psi.

The forging is then heat treated via a quenching process and allowed to cool before being machined into its final configuration. Once all machining is complete, the forged crank is heated to 400 to 600°F to relieve stress, and it is carefully allowed to cool. Then, final polishing and finish work are performed. It is the additional steps that make forged steel more expensive. Forged-steel crankshafts are typically made of 4340 hardened steel. Others are made of 1038 steel, which isn't as pure as 4340 but is still quite effective.

Tom Lieb, founder of Scat Enterprises, said that specialized formulas for forged-steel cranks vary from manufacturer to manufacturer. Scat's forging process differs from many manufacturers in that Scat uses a pressure technique instead of a traditional "slam-bam" hammer approach to make its forged-steel cranks. Instead of hammering molten 2,600°F metal into shape, it applies tremendous pressure to the near-fluid metal. Once the forging is trimmed and machined, it gets nitrided for good surface hardening. Few manufacturers have this process down to the degree that Scat does.

Scat has an edge because it manufactures some of the lightest crankshafts in the industry, which is what racers want. The lighter the crank (as well as rods and pistons), the faster your engine will rev. Eagle has its own unique approach to forged-steel crankshafts, which is a no-twist formula that comes from a special heat-treating and shot-peening process that ensures pinpoint accuracy at high RPM. Journals are cross-drilled and chamfered for a good oil wedge between the journal and bearing. A target bob weight of plus or minus 2 percent results in less balancing time with the Eagle crank.

Steel Billet

High-end billet crankshafts begin life as a solid cylindrical steel ingot, which enters a labor-intensive process of many CNC-machining steps before it looks like a crankshaft. The reason you would want a steel-billet crank is raw strength for the brutal environment of racing. It is the strongest crank that you can buy for a small-block engine, especially if you intend to spin it above 8,000 rpm, use nitrous oxide, turbocharge it, or supercharge it. The strength of a steel-billet crank comes from its one-piece nature and alloy makeup that has been machined into a crankshaft. Small-block Ford engines do not need a steel-billet crank for street/strip or bracket racing because it is purely a race piece for extreme-duty use.

Stroker Kits

The greatest power investment that can be made (aside from supercharging, turbocharging, or using nitrous oxide) is by increasing displacement. With displacement comes additional compression that can be dialed into your build. Displacement and compression remain the quickest paths to power. Keep compression conservative (around 10.0:1 on pump gas). You can stroke a stock 302 block to 347-plus ci. The 351W can be stroked to 427 ci.

Forty years ago, you needed a lot of imagination and talent to increase a small-block's stroke. You needed a seasoned crankshaft grinder who knew how to offset-grind the crank, or a good source, such as Scat Enterprises, to come up with a suitable stroker package. These days, many choices are available for 302/351W stroker kits. Select your series of stroker package wisely and don't waste valuable cash on parts that you don't need. A cast-steel crank, heavy-duty I-beam rods, and hypereutectic pistons work very well in a street/strip engine. With additional stroke and displacement, torque is abundant, which is important for street or weekend drag racing.

Scat Enterprises offers a broad range of cranks and stroker kits, including cast steel, forged, and billet. Cast steel is nodular iron (cast iron), which is the most affordable. Cast steel can tolerate 500 hp with the proper prep and treatment. Cast-steel cranks have a narrow parting line at the counterweights. Forged cranks have wider, more ragged parting lines.

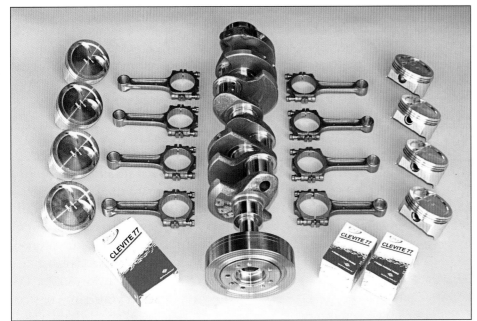

Before purchasing a stroker kit, thoroughly research your options. This is a middle-of-the-road stroker kit with a steel crank, I-beam rods with cap screw bolts, and forged pistons. The pistons are dished to control the compression ratio.

Offset weight is added at each end of the crank. These two flexplates (automatic transmission) have a welded-on offset weight. A 28-ounce offset flexplate (left) and a 50-ounce offset flexplate (right) are shown. Note the difference in counterweight size.

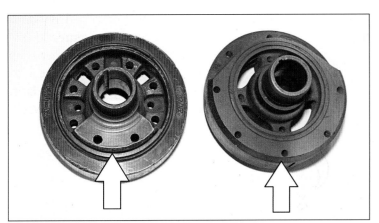

Small-block Fords are externally balanced engines, which means that the dynamic balancing needs help from both ends of the crank. Prior to 1982, offset balancing required 28 ounces of weight added to each end of the crank (left). From 1982 onward, the offset weight went to 50 ounces (right) to compensate for heavier rods.

Two basic types of harmonic dampers were used on small-block Fords: a three-bolt pulley and a four-bolt pulley. The three-bolt version (left) was used prior to 1970. The four-bolt version (right) is 1970–up. Keep this in mind because it affects your engine's front dress.

This flywheel (manual transmission) has a 28-ounce offset weight cast into the flywheel. A 50-ounce offset weight would be wider. The flywheel/flexplate and harmonic damper must be dynamically balanced with the crank, rods, bearings, pistons, and rings on an externally balanced engine.

If you are doing serious weekend or full-time drag or road racing, use a steel crank, heavy-duty I-beam or H-beam rods, and forged pistons. Use parts that can take the extremes of nitrous oxide, supercharging, or turbocharging. Any time that the power numbers are pushed beyond 500 hp without aided induction (nitrous oxide or a blower), seriously consider a steel crank, heavy-duty I-beam or H-beam rods, and forged pistons.

Building a Stroker

Ronnie Besselman of Bessel Motorsports suggested the following when shopping for a stroker kit.

- Use the longest connecting rod possible to minimize frictional losses and reduce side loading. This also allows more dwell time at each end of the bore for more power.
- Use the lightest bottom-end components possible, which frees up power and improves efficiency. However, don't sacrifice strength.
- Use a windage tray and pan that keep oil away from the crank and rods (windage). Effective lubrication is important. You don't want oil windage hindering power and efficiency.
- Remember that when you add stroke (displacement), you no longer have a 302 or a 351W. You have a higher-displacement 347- or 427-ci engine. Go with cylinder heads, a cam profile, and headers that are up to this increased displacement. Think larger.

- Be sure to tighten up the cam-lobe centerline to the optimal location by 1 degree for every 16 ci of increased displacement.
- Increase valve lift proportionately with displacement because you're moving more air through deeper bores.
- Increase induction capacity (go larger) to keep up with displacement.
- Keep the induction system cool with outside air.
- Step up header capacity (pipe size) at the primaries, secondaries, and collectors. Right-size your header tubes and exhaust pipes. If they're too large, torque is lost. If they're too small, horsepower is stifled.

Treat a stroker like a big-displacement engine because you now have 331 to 427 ci and all the power that goes with it. Cooling-system capacity must also increase along with induction, cylinder-head port/valve size, cam selection, and exhaust scavenging. Because of the ever-changing nature of stroker kits in a competitive marketplace, I can't list all the stroker kits there are available. However, when shopping for a stroker package, look to companies with an abundance of stroker-kit development and experience.

While shopping for a stroker kit, pay close attention to each of them and what their limitations are. What are your block's limitations? Will the crank counterweights and connecting rods clear the cylinder skirts, block webs, and pan rails? Much of this cannot be determined without doing a block mock-up to determine clearances. Cylinder skirts can be conservatively notched to clear

rod bolts. Pan rails and webs can be carefully shaved to clear crank counterweights. Crank counterweights or segments of the block can also be machined to clear the block by a seasoned machinist.

Strength in Stud Girdles

When studying the small-block's architecture, you will find that it has a good, healthy structure (depending upon your power requirements) but needs help underneath. The block is skirtless for weight reduction and ease of manufacturing, which robs the block of its strength.

Although the small-block yields strength for numbers upward of 400 hp, there's always room for an equalizer: the main stud girdle. Canton Racing offers the bolt-on main-cap girdle for the 302 and 351W to reinforce the main-cap alignment and to counter the limited main journal webbing in these skirtless blocks. It is machined to clear most stroker kits. It is not designed to clear stock pans.

Canton's main-cap support girdles are laser cut from 1/2- to 5/8-inch steel and offer CNC-machined mounting holes and rod notches for stroker kit clearance. It is one of the best means of support in the industry. These main-cap girdles bolt directly to the caps, eliminating the need for bushings, spacers, or unnecessary machining of the main caps for installation.

Danny's Speed Shop (D.S.S.) also offers a nice main cap girdle for the small-block Ford. The D.S.S. Support System features steel plates machined from 3/4-inch 6061 T6 billet aluminum, which beefs up the bottom end, virtually eliminating main-cap shift and annoying and destructive harmonics.

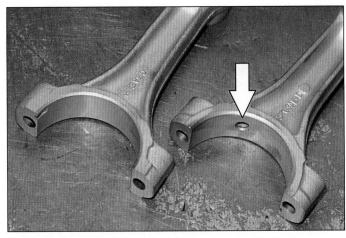

The C3AE rod forging, 5.155 inches in length, is shown. Early on, this rod was equipped with an oil-squirter hole (arrow) that sprayed hot oil under pressure on the cylinder wall. Ford engineers learned that there was sufficient oil splash from the crank and rod to the point that the oil jet wasn't necessary.

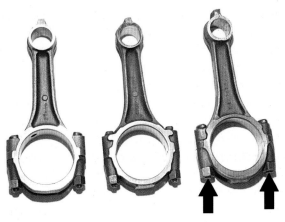

Three small-block Ford rods are shown (left to right): the C3AE rod for 221/260/289 engines (5.155 inches center to center), the C8OE rod for the 302/5.0L engines (5.090 inches), and the C3AE Boss 302 rod (5.155 inches). The first two have 5/16-inch bolts. The Boss 302 rod has more meat at the big end and larger 3/8-inch broached-head bolts.

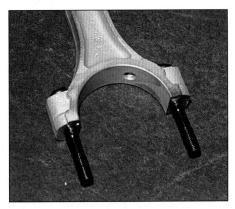

You can get away with stock Ford rods in a performance build. However, they should be shot-peened and nitrided for strength and fitted with ARP bolts to ensure durability. They can withstand up to 400 hp and 6,000 rpm.

The 302 engine's 5.090-inch C8OE rod (left) and the 351W's C9OE 5.596-inch rod (right) are shown.

Connecting Rods

The 221, 260, 289, 302, and 351W small-block engines have strong forged-steel connecting rods that experienced very few changes over their long production life. The 289 High Performance connecting rod is the same C3AE forging as the standard 289, with the exception

being that larger broached-head 3/8-inch rod bolts were pressed into a broached seat. Larger 3/8-inch bolts provide the integrity needed for high-RPM use.

When 289 rods are reconditioned, you have a choice between 5/16-inch or 3/8-inch ARP rod bolts, depending on how much material you have in the large end. If you can

get away with it, it is suggested that you go with 3/8-inch ARP bolts and shot-peened C3AE rods for strength and durability. Otherwise, you can get by with 5/16-inch ARP rod bolts that improve strength dramatically over stock.

The 221/260/289 rod is a 5.1545-inch (center to center) C3AE forging, while the 302 rod is a shorter 5.090-inch C8OE rod (as a means of identification). What is baffling to some degree is the Boss 302 rod. It is the same 5.1545-inch C3AE forging used in the 221/260/289 engines, with the exception being the use of 3/8-inch broached rod bolts and having more beef at the large end. The C3AE rod is slightly longer than a C8OE 302 rod, offering increased piston dwell time.

The shorter 302 rod forging is also common to 5.0L High Output engines, which received a heavier version of the C8OE rod. Aside from subtle changes to this rod at the large end (a thicker rod cap) to make it stronger for high-performance use, it is virtually the same rod. Always opt for a matched set of rods when you find them, mostly for reasons of balance and consistency.

One modification that you should make to both the C3AE and C8OE rods is to upgrade to ARP bolts for improved durability. Make sure that you have plenty of material around these bolts when this modification is made. Closely inspect each rod before pressing it into use.

The Boss 302 has a different piston than a 289 to achieve 302 ci and work with the Boss 302's poly-angle-valve 351C cylinder head with a high-dome wedge chamber match. There's also the hard-to-find Boss 302 Trans Am rod that is available with cap screw bolts (the C9ZE-G rod), which is on par with the Crower Sportsman or Scat Pro Series rod that is widely available. If you're building a Boss 302 to go vintage racing, you don't need to spend a fortune on a set of C9ZE-G cap-screw rods when the aftermarket offers a wealth of affordable rods for Boss 302 and 289 High Performance engines.

The 351W connecting rod is 5.956 inches center to center, regardless of block deck height. Throughout the 351W's long production life from 1969–1996, it employed the same basic connecting-rod forging with 3/8-inch bolts. You can recondition and shot-peen this rod. Then, fit it with 3/8-inch ARP bolts and end up with a rod that is good for up to 500 hp. In addition, you can do so with the stock 3M or 7M nodular iron crankshaft.

Aftermarket Connecting Rods

The automotive aftermarket offers a wealth of connecting-rod types for the small-block Ford. Scat

Scat's Pro Series I-beam rods, which are on a par with Crower Sportsman rods, are much stronger than stock rods but are affordable forgings that are a cut above stock replacement. A 5.400-inch Scat rod (left) and a shorter 5.090-inch rod are shown.

An I-beam rod (left) and a brute H-beam rod (right) are shown side by side. The Scat Pro Series I-beam rod has ARP 7/16-inch cap screw bolts. These rods are machined for cam clearance with strokers. In addition, they are shot-peened and stress-relieved for added strength. Dowel pins maintain perfect cap and rod alignment. The H-beam rod (right) is used for high-horsepower applications.

offers several different types of high-performance connecting rods, ranging from Pro Stock to Pro Sport. Scat connecting rods feature the same high-quality craftsmanship that has led the company to where it is today in the aftermarket industry. Scat rods are made from a two-piece chromoly-steel forging to ensure maximum strength and durability.

All Scat connecting rods are precision-machined and finished at Scat by master machinists on state-of-the-art equipment in the United States. The Scat Pro Stock I-beam rod is available in press-fit pin or bushed. This is a lightweight I-beam rod design to yield increased strength and quicker revs due to its lightweight design. In addition, Scat fits them with ARP Wave-Loc bolts for added security.

The Pro Sport H-beam rod is optimal for high-horsepower supercharged and nitrous-oxide applications, which makes it the strongest

Scat rod available. It has a special doweled cap for very specific cap-to-rod alignment.

I've covered several engine builds working with Eagle Specialties through the years. Eagle products have exceptional quality and precision. What you can't see on the surface of an Eagle rod is the material properties, quality control, precision machining, and attention to important details. This is why I've consistently worked with Eagle Specialties through the years. Eagle constantly purchases products from its competitors for physical and metallurgical tests to evaluate where it stands against its competition.

All Eagle H-beam rods are forged from certified 4340 chromoly steel. According to Eagle, not all 4340 steel is the same. To be classified as 4340 steel, certain alloy elements must be present in certain percentages. Specifications from Advanced Interior Solutions Inc. (AISI) and the Society of Automotive Engineers (SAE) call for 1.65-percent to 2.00-percent nickel content in 4340 steel. While this may appear to be a small difference, this is nearly an 18-percent variation. According to Eagle, 4340 steel with 1.65-percent nickel acts differently than 4340 steel with 2.00-percent nickel content. This is just one of many alloying elements involved in creating the right 4340 steel for Eagle rods.

The Procomp Electronics H-beam connecting rods are a nice rod for the money. They're good for supercharged and nitrous-oxide applications. They have a special dowel-pinned cap for very specific cap-to-rod alignment and are profiled with additional clearance for stroker applications. They are manufactured from 4340 chromoly steel with all surfaces shot-peened and stress-relieved.

Rod Ratio

When shopping for a stroker package, rod ratio should be a chief consideration—but not necessarily the only consideration. The rod ratio is determined by dividing the connecting-rod length by the stroke. The distance that a piston travels is cast in stone by the crankshaft stroke. How quickly it travels in each direction and how long it sits at each end of the bore is determined by connecting-rod length or rod ratio. The longer that a piston dwells, depending on cam profile, the more productive your fuel/air charge will be.

You want as much connecting rod as you can fit into the block without consequence (meaning excessive cylinder wall and bottom-end loading). With a longer connecting rod comes increased mechanical advantage. To determine the maximum amount of rod that you can get into a block, take the known compression height, divide the stroke length in half (actual crank-throw length), and subtract it from the block's deck height.

Piston Selection

Piston selection boils down to engine use. When planning an engine build, it is easy to go overboard and build more engine than you need. It is best to watch your money and build an engine as conservatively as possible based on what you know the engine will do.

If you're building a daily driver, weekend cruiser, or tow vehicle, you don't need a steel crank, H-beam

This is a stock Boss 302 forged piston with a Ford part number (D0ZE-61110-A). The issue with these OEM pistons was skirt failure, which was why there were Boss 302 engine failures and service-replacement blocks and engines. If you're building a "Clevor" engine (a 289/302/351W with 351C heads), use a special piston with a raised dome, such as this one. Off-the-shelf pistons are available from the aftermarket for Clevor builds.

The question about piston type (cast, hypereutectic, or forged) often arises. The choice depends on the engine's intended use. For street use and cruising (300 to 400 hp), you can get away with cast or hypereutectic. Hypereutectic is a fancy word for high-silicon cast piston. What makes hypereutectic better than cast is the added strength without the penalty of the expansion issues that occur with forged pistons. Forged pistons have a greater expansion rate than cast. They rattle on cold starts.

A stock piston (left) and a stroker piston (right) are shown. The pin gets pushed up just short of the ring lands. There's less skirt with a stroker piston.

When the stroke is increased, cylinder volume is increased, which results in greater compression. When you order a stroker kit, the manufacturer needs to know details about your engine and how it will be configured. We dish the stroker piston to control compression. If you're going to supercharge or turbocharge the engine or run nitrous oxide, even greater consideration must be paid to cylinder volume and compression ratio.

rods, and forged pistons. Even if you intend to spin the engine to 6,500 rpm on occasion, you can get away with a cast crank, stock shot-peened rods with ARP bolts, and cast or hypereutectic pistons.

Hypereutectic pistons are a nice compromise between cast and forged. Although the word "hypereutectic" sounds high tech, the process has been around since 1902. A Hypereutectic piston is a high-silicon cast piston that is made of a harder cast material but without the expansion issues of forged pistons. Hypereutectic pistons are more durable than cast without the high price tag or the expansion issues.

Cast pistons are the most basic type of piston that you can stuff into an engine. Because I've used Mahle pistons extensively through the years, I suggest considering Mahle across the board for your mild street or all-out race build. The Mahle Ecoform cast piston is designed for modern engine building. It is a lighter piston due to fresh casting technol-ogy, and it is more durable than the average cast piece.

According to Trey McFarland of Mahle Pistons, "Our cast Ecoform pistons are 20- to 25-percent lighter than the cast pistons that we were making 16 years ago."

This feature enables you to get good throttle response from your engine because there's less recipro-cating weight. All cast pistons have a certain amount of silicon (sand) in them for strength and hardness. However, cast pistons are also brittle and can't take the kind of extreme shock loads and heat that forged race pistons can. This is where you need to know up front how you're going to use your small-block. What you get from a cast piston is stability, pre-dictable expansion properties, and quiet cold operation.

Although cast pistons have their place, I suggest using hypereutectic pistons as a base-piston selection for any engine build because they are more durable than cast and don't have the expansion issues of forged pistons. As I understand it from those who design and manufacture pistons, cast pistons have roughly 10-percent silicon in the aluminum alloy. Hypereutectic pistons have higher amounts of silicon, which calls for heat treating to the point that the silicon blends into the alu-minum to create a harder surface.

Forged pistons cost consider-ably more because they call for more manufacturing steps to get a finished product. Once piston forgings are slammed (forged) into shape under very high pressure, they must be machined through a series of com-plex steps.

Forged pistons are more chal-lenging to produce because of what the machinist has to think about during the block-machining process. Because forged pistons possess greater expansion properties, the machinist must allow for this in how cylinders are bored and honed to size. There must be sufficient piston-to-cylinder-wall clearances. You can't hone a bore to the same dimensions as you would for cast or hypereutectic pistons because forged pistons expand at a different rate.

The first company to develop forged pistons was Federal-Mogul's Sealed Power division in the 1960s. There was a learning curve (like we saw with the Boss 302 engine in 1969–1970), with cracked piston skirts and other failure issues that caused warranty headaches and engine replacements. Sealed Power developed forged pistons using the VMS75 aluminum alloy, which has been a factory piston alloy for ages.

The automotive aftermarket industry utilizes the 2618 alloy for race pistons with great success because it can withstand up to 575°F. One shortcoming of 2618 is hardness. It isn't as hard as another widely used alloy that is known as 4032, which has higher amounts of silicon, making aluminum alloys very hard. The 4032 piston makes more sense for street and racing use.

Selecting a piston evolves from material to dimensions, which can get tricky if you don't know what you're doing. This is why you want to be completely sure about the crank throw, block deck height, compression height, and more. It is easy to get this wrong and end up with pistons that don't fit. This is why you must first select a crank and rod before settling on a piston. Manufacturers make this easier because engine kits typically include pistons.

Harmonic Dampers and Flywheels

Harmonic dampers are generally elastomeric with an outer ring that is separated from the inner hub by a rubber shock band. Because several types of small-block Ford engines exist, determine what you have before ordering a flywheel/flexplate and harmonic damper. There is the three-bolt harmonic damper prior to 1970 and the four-bolt harmonic damper from 1970 onward. There's also the issue of 28-ounce offset balance (prior to 1982) versus the 50-ounce offset balance from 1982 onward.

The harmonic damper damps the destructive vibration of a spinning, pulsing crankshaft and absorbs torsional stresses from combustion pulses. Torsional stress and vibration come from torque placed on the crank as each piston rises on the compression/ignition stroke and the light-off exerts force on each journal.

The piston and rod not only bump against compression stroke but they also bounce off compression with combustion and linear force. Because this happens in rapid succession even at idle, it sets up a harmonic that is known as resonance. Resonance is

The most widely used aftermarket damper is the ATI Super Damper. The ATI Super Damper can be rebuilt and reused. This patented design is the only design that is exclusively for high-performance Ford small-block engines. It eliminates torsional crankshaft vibrations; exceeds SFI 18.1 specs; is tunable, rebuildable, and extremely efficient at all RPM ranges; and is laser etched so the timing marks never wear off.

The biggest issue with strokers is clearances. During a preassembly mock-up, clearances with the block, cylinder skirts, camshaft, and stud girdles must all be checked. At least 0.100 inch of clearance is needed between the crank, rods, and those components. Check the pan and oil-pump clearances as well.

When building a stroker, check to ensure that you have a cam base circle that will clear the reciprocating mass moving up and down in the cylinder bore. The rod must clear the cam's base circle. This is a normal-base-circle camshaft.

tle. The harmonic balancer absorbs destructive resonance by allowing a soft rebound with each combustion pulse.

Harmonic dampers normally have two components that are designed to absorb vibration and help momentum. The outer ring and rubber elastomeric band absorb shock and are mounted on a hub that is fitted over the end of the crank. The crank can twist as much as 1 to 2 degrees at wide-open throttle, which is a lot of twist.

Harmonic damper choice depends on how you intend to use the engine, said Jim "JC" Beattie of ATI Performance. First, he asks about the application for the engine. Cast cranks normally absorb more low-range torsionals (twist) on a low-RPM engine that makes a lot of torque. A forged-steel or a steel-billet crank will live longer and take more horsepower and high RPM where a cast crank is less tolerant.

Some sanctioning racing organizations, such as NASCAR and the National Hot Rod Association (NHRA), do not allow aluminum dampers or related parts for safety reasons. Steel dampers are the only choice for road and circle-track racing. It is important to confirm before ordering a damper.

Street engines need little more than a stock damper. If you plan to drive at high RPM, use an SFI-approved balancer that has been engineered to stay together at high RPM. ATI Performance pioneered the race-ready harmonic damper. Each type of ATI damper is engineered for a specific engine family based on research and development time for each type. Harmonic balancers damp the "spring" effect of an engine's crankshaft.

that weird flutter that you hear when two race cars roar down the track at the same time to create a musical harmony. The same thing happens to a crankshaft as well as other parts in the engine, especially at full throt-

Dynamic balancing is a must. Pistons, rods, rings, bearings, and even engine oil are weighed and weighted to the lightest set. Each is machined to the weight of the lightest assembly. Bobweights (white arrows) are weighted to that lightest assembly and bolted to each of the rod journals. Because the small-block Ford is externally balanced, the flywheel and harmonic damper must be bolted to the crank during balancing.

Dynamic Balancing

All small-blocks (stock or modified) should be dynamically balanced for smoothness and durability. Dynamic balancing means getting reciprocating mass (pistons, rings, rod bearings, connecting rods, and oil) to the exact same weight as the crankshaft counterweights. This enables the reciprocating mass and crankshaft counterweights to move around each other in perfect unison with great smoothness. No one wants an engine that shakes. Vibration is a destructive dynamic that shortens engine life.

When shopping engine kits, ask if the components have been dynamically balanced. If you are told they're "Detroit balanced" or just "balanced," that's not enough. Detroit balancing is what the automakers use in production engine building, which means pistons, rods, and related parts are grouped in lots with similar weights and thrown together, which is passable with production engines but not acceptable with an expensive engine build. Your engine should rev smoothly and without destructive vibration.

Balancing begins with getting the reciprocating weight uniform with the lightest piston-and-rod assembly and all of the related parts. If cylinder number-7 is the lightest piston-and-rod assembly, all reciprocating units must be shaved down to that exact weight. Then, all crankshaft counterweights must weigh that same amount. Externally balanced engines must have flywheels/flexplates that are balanced with the crank and reciprocating assemblies.

Revco Precision Balancing in Long Beach, California, has performed a lot of dynamic balancing for engine build projects that I've been involved with. Larry Revis of Revco explained that this art focuses on balancing, vibration analysis, and specialty machine work on engines and machines. He stressed close attention to detail in dynamic balancing and burning the midnight oil until the process is perfected. Some balancing jobs can be decidedly frustrating and take much longer than anticipated, he said. The result is what engine builders must focus on to achieve unending smoothness.

Balancing can sometimes involve adding Mallory metal (tungsten) to the counterweights. This happens when it is decided that the engine will be internally balanced, where the balancing is handled inside the engine and there's no need for external balance. External balancing is where offset weights (28 ounce or 50 ounce) are added at each end of the crankshaft.

LUBRICATION

Lubrication is a necessity for an engine's survival. Oil under pressure keeps moving parts apart with a solid oil wedge and out of harm's way. In addition, oil acts as a coolant because it has the most intimate contact with the engine's hottest parts, such as valve stems and guides. The more that an engine's lubrication system can be improved, the more durability it will have.

First, some understanding of how the small-block Ford's oiling system works is required. The positive-displacement "gerotor" oil pump draws oil from the pan sump and pumps it up to the oil filter, where it passes through a filter mesh into the main oil gallery to the right-hand side of the camshaft. The pump is driven through a shaft off the distributor gear, which is driven by the camshaft.

The main oil gallery feeds oil that is under pressure to the main crankshaft journals via drilled passages in the block. Passages are drilled from each main-bearing journal to each cam journal. The number-1 main journal feeds oil to the number-1 cam journal and so on through number-5. Oil then flows from notches or grooves in the main crank-

shaft bearings. The timing chain and sprockets in front are lubricated from the number-1 camshaft bearing. The crankshaft is drilled from the main journals to the rod journals to lubricate the rod bearings and journals.

A small groove is located in the connecting rod at the mating face where the cap meets with the rod. This groove enables oil to be slung onto the opposite cylinder wall for lubrication. The number-1 rod slings oil onto the number-5 cylinder wall. The number-2 rod slings oil onto number-6 and so on.

Oil passages are drilled from the main oil gallery to each lifter gallery on each side of the camshaft for each side of the block. Oil under pressure feeds each of the lifters. Oil pressure not only lubricates each of the lifters but also maintains valve lash in each lifter. As a rule, the small-block oiling system ensures that there's plenty of

Begin the oiling system build with a high-volume Melling oil pump. These are solid, dependable pumps with exceptional quality. They deliver volume, which is what you want from an oil pump, along with 10 psi per 1,000 rpm. They require close inspection and blueprinting much as the rest of the engine.

Blueprinting the oiling system includes chasing all of the oil galleries with a bottle brush and ball hone to work the galleries clean. After chasing the oil galleries, flush them thoroughly with soapy water. Then, use a high-evaporative solvent, such as brake cleaner, and compressed air to chase any remaining debris.

Install screw-in oil gallery plugs at the gallery ends behind the cam sprocket. These offer better oiling-system security than the factory pressed-in plugs.

Two oil galleries are at the main saddle: one from the oil filter and pump (left arrow) and another (right arrow) up to the cam journals. Note the crisp crossmatch pattern in this main saddle, which is there to help main bearing security.

MCE Engines suggests the use of restrictors between the main and cam journals to keep more oil around the main bearings.

You may not think of this as the oiling system. However, lifter bores should be honed to a crosshatch pattern to improve oil flow around the lifters and maintain oil pressure.

Massage all oil gallery passages to reduce fluid turbulence.

Begin your oiling system blueprinting with the best oil pump possible. Melling pumps have solid integrity. Never use the stock oil-pump shaft, even if you're building a mild street engine. Order the ARP shaft.

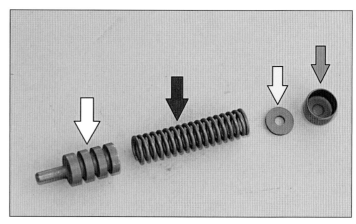

The relief-valve parts are laid out in proper order. The relief-valve piston, or plunger (white arrow), does the actual regulating of pressure. The spring (red arrow) holds pressure against the piston. The shim (yellow arrow) controls spring pressure via thickness, and the end cap (blue arrow) is on the far right.

Carefully disassemble the pump, taking note of where everything goes. Lay out the parts in proper order. Here, the pressure-relief valve is removed using an Allen wrench.

The relief-valve bore can be honed (as shown) if the relief-valve piston clearance is tight. The piston should move freely in the bore.

oil going to all of the moving parts.

The most common oiling system issue is a loss of oil pressure. Oil-pressure problems are not always due to the oil pump itself. Instead, a loss of oil pressure is normally an issue beyond the pump. Pumps can break off and fall into the pan, or they may lose the relief valve parts and pump oil back into the sump (instead of going to important moving parts). In addition, pump shafts can shear, especially if you're run-

ning a stock pump shaft, which is why you shouldn't use a stock pump shaft even with a stock engine. You must use a high-volume oil pump. Melling is your best choice, followed by a thorough blueprinting prior to installation.

The biggest reasons for an oil-system failure include using incorrect lifters and roller lifters being installed backward so that the oil hole in the lifter is aligned with the main oil gallery. This causes oil to

be pumped up the pushrods, flooding the top end and running the pan dry. When this happens, the engine's most important parts don't receive lubrication.

Another problem that I've seen is with the pickup bolts and flange at the oil pump. The pickup can develop leaks at this joint and draw in air, making the oil foamy, which hurts the oil wedge at the moving parts. The pickup flange isn't always robust enough to remain attached

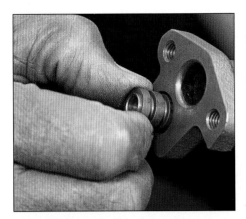

The relief valve's freedom of movement is demonstrated. Use engine oil or WD-40 when you're checking movement.

Blueprinting an oil pump involves chamfering ragged edges that can cause turbulence. Carefully chamfering the edges smooths out the flow.

Both the plate and pump housing are "milled" on a perfectly flat surface with 400-grit paper to perfect the surfaces. Do this only when end clearances are excessive. You can use plate glass for a perfect surface or milled stone.

Rotor end clearance is checked (as shown) and should be 0.0011 to 0.0041 inch using a simple thickness gauge between the plate and rotor.

to the pump. With the original Ford oil pickups, this has rarely been an issue. Aftermarket stock replacement pickups are at times lame enough to become detached. Use the thickest flange that you can find. Always use Grade-8 bolts to attach the pickup.

Oil pressure can also suffer from excessive bearing clearances or a forgotten oil gallery plug. If the forgotten plug is external, you will have seven quarts of engine oil on the garage floor.

The small-block Ford's oiling system can be improved by using a blueprinted high-volume pump and cleaning the oil galleries where possible to reduce turbulence and restriction. You want the most volume possible as well as a good return flow to the pan. A windage tray and a baffled pan will keep the oil around the pickup during hard cornering and acceleration. Select the most oil-pan capacity without going overboard.

Even if you're building a mild street performance engine, choose a baffled Boss 302 oil pan that has been designed to keep oil around the pickup during hard cornering and acceleration. Road racing applications call for a T-pan with doors and baffles that keep oil around the pickup during hard cornering. Drag-racing applications call for a deep-sump pan because that's where the oil goes during hard acceleration. Plenty of oil must be on hand in the sump under hard acceleration.

When blueprinting an engine, make sure that everything is blueprinted. Chamfer not only the crank-journal oil passages but also every oil gallery. Oil should flow smoothly through all of the galleries without turbulence at the transition points. Take a small ball hone and run it through the block galleries to make the ride smooth for the engine's lubrication.

Install screw-in oil gallery plugs at the front of the block during machine work. The factory-installed, pressed-in oil-gallery plugs could pop out at high RPM. Do this even with a stock build. One builder who I have worked with recommends drilling a 0.020-inch oil hole in the right-hand lifter-gallery plug to help lubricate the chain assembly.

While blueprinting the oiling system, keep drainback in mind. Install screening at all drainback points in the heads and lifter valley to keep destructive debris out of the oil pan. Even the smallest debris can do extensive engine damage if it

This is another way to check rotor end clearance with a clearance gauge, which checks clearances between the rotor and housing end.

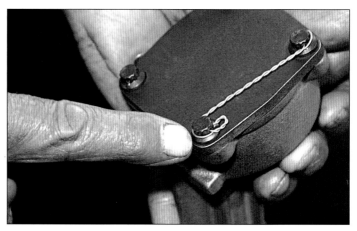

Use threadlocker on bolt threads or use safety wiring to connect the bolt heads to each other to ensure bolt security.

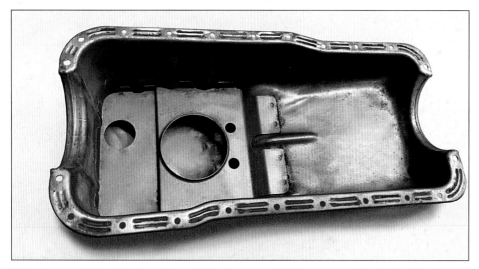

This is an original factory Boss 302 oil pan, which is appropriately baffled to keep oil around the pickup in the sump. Scott Drake/Holley offers a Boss 302 pan like this one, which is a good investment even for a warmed-up street/strip build.

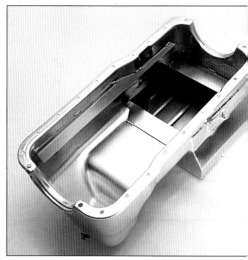

Fox Body Mustangs are fitted with a double-sump oil pan because the main sump is located aft of the front subframe. The pickup is in the rear sump, connected to the oil pump in the front sump by a long tube. This is a deep-sump, drag-race pan that was designed to keep oil in the sump during hard acceleration.

Windage trays, which keep sump oil out of the spinning crank, are available from a variety of aftermarket companies. This provides a shield between the crank and oil to reduce the risk of pump cavitation.

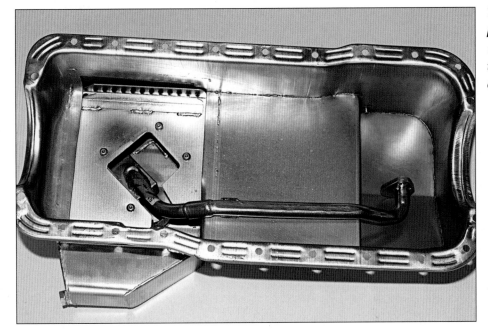

This is a Fox Body Mustang road-race pan with the pump sump in front (right) and baffled main sump (left) in the rear to keep oil around the pickup during hard cornering.

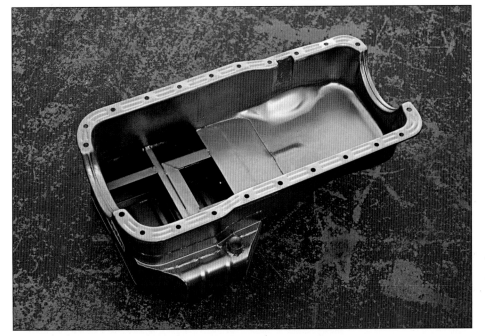

This is a Milodon front-sump, road-race pan with baffling and doors that keep oil around the pickup during hard cornering.

check: gerotor endplay, radial clearances for a full 360 degrees, and the pressure-relief valve function/spring pressure. If the pressure-relief valve piston binds in any way as you press it in, chase the bore with a small ball hone until the piston glides smoothly with lubrication. If radial clearances are tight, have a machine shop examine and bore them as necessary or return the pump to the manufacturer. Rotor end clearances must fall somewhere between the minimum and maximum that is allowable. If there's too much clearance, you can have the housing milled to size or you can return the pump and hope for a better core.

JGM Performance Engineering religiously hones lifter bores to get a nice finish hone, which controls oil flow around the lifters. This controls oil pressure. It also chamfers oil holes in the crank to improve flow across the main and rod bearings. JMG also carefully watches bearing clearances.

Oil-Pump Tolerances	
Relief Valve-Spring Tension	11.15 to 11.75 ft-lbs at 1.704 inches
Relief Valve Piston Clearance	0.0015 to 0.0029 inch
Drive Shaft to Housing Bearing Clearance	0.0015 to 0.0029 inch
Rotor Assembly End Clearance	0.0011 to 0.0041 inch
Outer Rotor Race to Housing Clearance	0.006 to 0.012 inch

makes its way through the oil pickup and through the pump.

The late Marvin McAfee of MCE Engines was very methodical in his engine builds. McAfee stressed that oil pumps must never be installed right out of the box. Most engine builders install oil pumps right out

of the box, assuming that all of the bases have been covered. However, they can come out of the box with flaws and machining errors. Unless you inspect them and measure critical clearances, you're rolling the dice with your oiling system.

There are three oil-pump items to

CYLINDER HEADS

Cylinder-head selection for the small-block Ford is complex because many factory castings exist between 1962 and 2000. However, there aren't many differences across the board in these castings. Over the half-century production life of the small-block Ford, dozens of various cylinder head castings were produced. Some are desirable castings, and some are throwaways.

Ford is notorious for lame factory cylinder-head port sizing. These small-block heads never had sufficient breathing qualities, which limited performance. We used to take 351W heads and put them on a 289/302 to gain breathability and power. However, for what was gained with larger ports and marginal breathing was lost in compression because the 351W head had larger chambers, which hurt compression. The 351W head only became worse with time, tougher emissions standards, and larger chambers. The 351W engine was later fitted with the 302 cylinder head from the factory to reduce production costs.

Because the aftermarket offers a wealth of cylinder-head choices today, there's little reason to use a factory head. If you are seeking a stock appearance, you may be limited to factory heads, in which case there are some solutions. You can have port work done and larger valves installed (1.940-inch intake and 1.600-inch exhaust). You may opt for early 1969–1971 351W heads with port work and the appropriate pistons to bump compression. This keeps your 289/302 stock stealthy in appearance while turning up the flame at the wheels.

First, let's first dissolve some myths that surround small-block Ford cylinder heads. Aside from valve-spring pockets and screw-in rocker-arm studs, there is no difference between the 289/302 2V/4V head and the 289

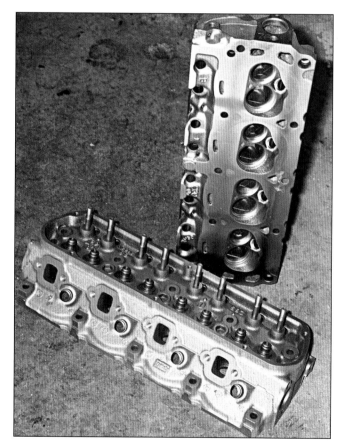

Stock 260/289 heads never excelled regarding the flow rate or port sizing. These cylinder heads prior to 1968 employed the smallest 53- to 57-cc chambers, which offered the greatest quench and compression. However, these heads suffer from very restrictive ports and valve sizing. Prior to May 8, 1966 (casting date code), these head castings had cast-in pushrod guides. From May 8, 1966, onward, Ford went to a rail-style rocker arm, which didn't need guides cast into the head.

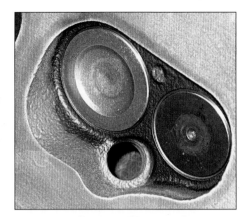

These small 53- to 57-cc wedge chambers offer the greatest compression and quench.

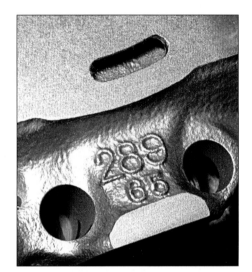

Small-block head castings are typically easily identified with displacement and model year. In this case, the head is from a 1965 289-ci engine.

The Ford casting number of "C5AE" indicates the calendar year and engineering level. This doesn't necessarily mean that it came from a 1965 Ford or Mercury. It indicates the engineering level of the casting and the year that it was released. If the casting isn't revised, the basic casting number does not change.

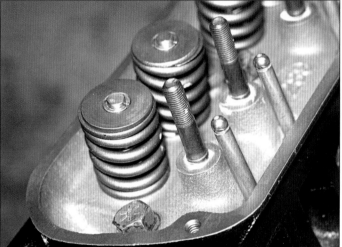

Stock 289/302/351W heads have pressed-in rocker-arm studs. The rocker-arm studs shown here are screw-in studs that are void of a hex head but are still screw-in studs. If you intend to run a high-lift cam, screw-in studs are required. Otherwise, pressed-in studs can pull out of the head due to higher valve-spring pressure.

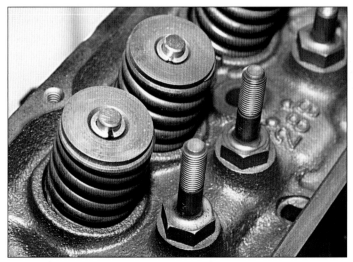

The 289 High Performance V-8 was factory-equipped with screw-in rocker-arm studs. You can do this with any 289/302/351W head in the interest of valvetrain security.

High Performance head casting. Port and valve size are the same, as are the chambers, which average 53 to 57 cc through 1967. Stay away from heads beyond 1967. They suffer from larger chambers and reduced compression.

The 289 Hi-Po heads from 1963–1967 have a few variations. The 289 High Performance service head with a 1968 casting number has slightly larger ports but valve and chamber size remain the same. There are

The 289 High Performance head has the same size of intake ports as a regular 260/289/302 head casting.

You typically see "4V" on a 289 High Performance head. However, that's not the case with the 2V/4V head.

around an "F" stands for the Cleveland foundry and 2) "WF" or "WC" stands for the Windsor foundry or Windsor Casting.

This 302 head casting has a single dot. The 302 head casting has larger 63- to 64-cc chambers, which hinders compression. Two forms of foundry indication are present on these 260/289/302 head castings: 1) this circling "C"

As 289/302 production progressed into the late 1960s, chambers became larger for reduced emissions. This is a 1969 302 truck-head chamber in the 64- to 67-cc range. With a larger chamber and flat-top pistons comes reduced compression.

exceptions out there—obscure castings (some experimental) that some people have seen at swap meets and machine shops. Experimental heads are identified by the casting number.

The 1968 302-4V head is the one to grab if you're looking for a stock appearance while getting more compression for your money via smaller 53-cc chambers. The quickest path (and cheapest) to power is increasing the compression ratio. This is likely one of the rarest small-block heads out there.

The biggest myth is regarding the 351W head. It has never been exceptional. From 1969 to 1971, you get a head with larger ports, and larger valves, and a 64-cc chamber. This is a casting that you can work with by doing some port work and opting for the largest valve that you can put into these chambers. Otherwise, the 351W head isn't your best option. In addition, for all of the cash that you can sink into the factory cast-iron 351W head, your money would be better used by investing in aftermarket aluminum heads.

This is a 1975 vintage 351W head with smaller 14-mm spark-plug holes and larger chambers. Ideally, you will find a 1969–1971 head casting with smaller chambers, easily identified by their larger 18-mm spark-plug holes.

This is a 1969–1974 351W chamber, which is more shovel shaped, with the 18-mm spark-plug hole. The 1972–1973 head has induction-hardened exhaust-valve seats for use with unleaded fuels. This head has been CNC and hand ported.

The 351W head is easily identified by the "351" and "WCP" for Windsor Casting Plant. By 1978, Ford was installing 302 heads on 351W engines due to cost, and it really didn't matter. It had little effect on performance.

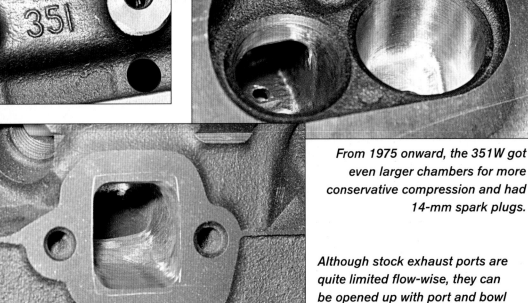

From 1975 onward, the 351W got even larger chambers for more conservative compression and had 14-mm spark plugs.

Although stock exhaust ports are quite limited flow-wise, they can be opened up with port and bowl work to improve scavenging. Unless you're building a stocker, it makes more economic sense to use after-market heads.

All engine builds should include screw-in rocker-arm studs—even if you're building a mild stocker, which improves durability. Viton valve seals are the only choice when it comes to valve seals. Valve guides have to be machined to accommodate the Viton seals, which offer better oil control and sealing.

255: The Misfit

The only small-block Ford that is impossible to recommend is the 255-ci V-8 (4.2L) that was produced from 1980 to 1982. Ford reduced the 302's 4.000-inch bore to 3.680 inches and kept the same 3.000-inch stroke to get 255 ci and satisfy federally mandated Corporate Average Fuel Economy (CAFE) numbers.

The 255 head (E0SE-AB), with its 53- to 56-cc chambers and 1.680/1.460-inch valves, is a unique casting with small, round, restrictive intake ports to improve emissions and fuel economy. Although a number of 1980–1982 Mustangs were produced with this engine, it was not conceived with performance in mind. It is strictly an emissions engine, as there are plenty of 302 cores out there that you can build instead.

1968 302 Tunnel Port

There is always some confusion when Ford enthusiasts discuss the rare 302 Tunnel Port cylinder head, which was produced only in 1968 strictly for SCCA Trans-Am racing purposes. The Tunnel Port was never installed on a production 302-4V engine. The 302 High Performance Tunnel Port cylinder head turned out to be a public-relations disaster for Ford because racers had to push the 302 beyond its limits (8,000 to 9,000 rpm) to make the power that was necessary to win races.

Bill Barr, who was in charge of the Boss 302 program, told me that Ford stressed to racers not to push this engine to the extreme. Racers did what racers do, and these engines failed with great regularity before reaching the finish line.

The 302 Tunnel Port head had shaft-style adjustable rocker arms to handle the RPM range that was expected. Intake ports were huge with pushrod tubes traveling through the middle of each port like the FE-series 427 Tunnel Port big-block. In 1969 and beyond, Ford's high-revving small-block Boss engines led Ford to the winner's circle in SCCA Trans-Am competition.

Boss 302

In the wake of interviews with retired Ford engineer Bill Barr, the Boss 302 came from raw necessity— the need for a cylinder head that would perform and make winning power below 8,000 rpm. Searching for viable solutions, Bill walked over to Advanced Engines to look at the 351C engine that was in development at the time. He looked at the all-new Cleveland block and heads and noticed that the bolt spacing was the same as the 289/302/351W. This meant that the 351C-4V head (with its large ports, wedge chambers, and poly-angle valves) would fit the 302/351W block. The Boss 302 was born.

The Boss 302 cylinder head is little more than a 351C-4V head casting with revised cooling passages that make it compatible with the 289/302/351W block. Of course, everyone knows this, but it was nice to hear it straight from the horse's mouth. Because the 351C has a dry intake manifold, where coolant is routed through the block and heads instead of the intake manifold, the Boss head had to be factory machined to route coolant through the intake manifold instead of the block and heads exclusively. This was an easy modification to make to an existing head casting and could easily be accomplished in production.

Based on what I've seen in 40 years of Ford engine builds, it appears that early Boss 302 heads were cast at the Windsor foundry. Otherwise, they were cast at Cleveland. Which Boss head to use depends on what you want from your Boss 302 engine. The 1969 Boss 302 head has larger valves that deliver better high-RPM breathing but hinder low-end torque, which makes it frustrating for street use. The 1970 head employs more conservative valve sizing, which makes it more street friendly.

Cylinder Head Identification (221, 260, 289, 302, 351W, and Boss 302)

Displacement	Year	Casting/Part Number	Chamber Size (cc)	Valve Size (Intake/Exhaust)	Port Size (Intake/Exhaust)
221 ci	1962–1963	C2OE-A, C2OE-B, C2OE-C, C2OE-D, C2OE-E, C3OE-A	45–41	1.590/1.390 inches	1.76 x 1.00 inches, 1.24 x 1.00 inches
255 ci	1980–1982	E0SE-AB	53.6–56.0	1.680/1.460 inches	N/A
260 ci	1962–1963	C2OE-F, C3OE-B	52–55	1.590/1.390 inches	1.76 x 1.00 inches, 1.24 x 1.00 inches
260 ci	1964	C4OE-B (Revised 260 head)	52–55	1.670/1.450 inches	1.76 x 1.00 inches, 1.24 x 1.00 inches
289 ci	1963	C3AE-F, C3OE-E, C3OE-F	52–55	1.670/1.450 inches	1.76 x 1.00 inches, 1.24 x 1.00 inches
289 ci	1964	C4AE-C (Revised 289 head)	52–55	1.780/1.450 inches	1.76 x 1.00 inches, 1.24 x 1.00 inches
289 ci	1965–1966	C5DE-B, C6DE-G, C6OE-C (Thermactor), C6OE-E (Thermactor), C6OE-M	52–55 (C5DE-B, C6DE-G, C6OE-C, C6OE-E), 63 (C6OE-M)	1.780/1.450 inches	1.76 x 1.00 inches, 1.24 x 1.00 inches
289 ci	1967–1968	C7OE-A (Thermactor), C7OE-B (Thermactor), C7OE-C, C7OZ-B (Thermactor), C7ZE-A (Thermactor), C8OE-D (Thermactor), C8OE-L (Thermactor), C8OE-M (Thermactor)	63	1.780/1.450 inches	1.94 x 1.04 inches, 1.24 x 1.00 inches
289 ci	1963	C3OE (High Performance)	52–55	1.670/1.450 inches	1.94 x 1.04 inches, 1.24 x 1.00 inches
289 ci	1964–1967	C4OE-B, C5OE-A (High Performance), C5AE-E, C7ZZ-B (Service Head)	52–55	1.780/1.450 inches	1.94 x 1.04 inches, 1.24 x 1.00 inches
302 ci	1968–1978	C7OE-C, C7OE-G, C8OE-F (1968 302-ci 4V head), C8OE-J, C8OE-K (Thermactor), C8OE-L (Thermactor), C8OE-M, C8AE-J, C8DE-F, C9TE-C (Truck Head), D0OE-B, D1TZ-A (Truck Head), D2OE-GA, D5OE-A3A, D5OE-A3B, D7OE-DA	63 (C7OE-C, C7OE-G), 53.5 (C8OE-F), 63 (C8OE-J), 58.2 (C8OE-K, C8OE-L), 63 (C8OE-M, C8AE-J, C8DE-F), 69 (C9TE-C), N/A (D0OE-B, D1TZ-A, D2OE-GA, D5OE-A3A, D5OE-A3B, D7OE-DA)	1.780/1.450 inches	1.94 x 1.04 inches, 1.24 x 1.00 inches
302 ci 1979–1984	1979–1984	D9AE-AA	67.5–70	1.780/1.450 inches	1.94 x 1.04 inches, 1.24 x 1.00 inches
302 ci (5.0L) High Output 4V	1985	E5AE-CA	67–70	1.780/1.450 inches	1.94 x 1.04 inches, 1.24 x 1.00 inches
302 ci (5.0L) High Output	1986	E6AE-AA	62–65	1.780/1.450 inches	1.94 x 1.04 inches, 1.24 x 1.00 inches
302 ci (5.0L) High Output	1987–1993	E5TE-PA, E7TE-PA	62–65	1.780/1.450 inches	1.94 x 1.04 inches, 1.24 x 1.00 inches
302 ci (5.0L) Cobra	1993	F3ZE-AA	60–63	1.840/1.540 inches	N/A
302 ci (5.0L) Cobra	1994–1995	F4ZE-AA	60–63	1.840/1.540 inches	N/A
302 ci (5.0L) Explorer, Mountaineer, GT40P	1996–1997	F1ZE-AA	63–66	1.840/1.540 inches	N/A
302ci (5.0L) Explorer, Mountaineer, GT40P	1997–2000	F7ZE-AA	58–61	1.840/1.540 inches	N/A
Boss 302	1969	C9ZE-A, C9ZE-C	61–64	2.230/1.710 inches	2.50 x 1.75 inches, 2.00 x 1.74 inches
Boss 302	1970	D0ZE-A, D1ZE-A (Service Head)	58	2.190/1.710 inches	2.50 x 1.75 inches, 2.00 x 1.74 inches
351W	1969–1984	C9OE-B, C9OE-D, D0OE-C, D0OE-G, D5TE-EB (Truck Head), D7OE-A, D8OE-A, D8OE-AB	60 (C9OE-B, C9OE-D, D0OE-C, D0OE-G), 69 (D5TE-EB, D7OE-A, D8OE-A, D8OE-AB)	1.840/1.540 inches	1.94 x 1.04 inches, 1.24 x 1.00 inches
351W	1985–1986	E5AE-CA	67–70	1.780/1.450 inches	1.94 x 1.04 inches, 1.24 x 1.00 inches
351W	1987–1995	E7TE-PA (Truck Head)	62–65	1.780/1.450 inches	1.94 x 1.04 inches, 1.24 x 1.00 inches

Aftermarket Cylinder Heads

Forty years ago, builders had to use factory iron heads. Today, the aftermarket delivers a strong lineup of terrific iron and aluminum cylinder heads. Aluminum is the best option due to its heat conductivity and the engineering that goes into these heads in a very competitive market.

Look at every aspect of a cylinder head: the port and valve sizing as well as the chamber size and shape. You can have larger valves, but is valve shrouding an issue? Tight valve shrouding limits air and exhaust-gas flow. Watch out for large valves and critical clearances in both the chamber and between valve and piston. Chamber size affects compression. A 64- to 67-cc chamber on a 289 or 302 can lose compression to the point that there's no benefit to using the head. If you run nitrous oxide or forced induction, chamber size is critical there too because compression has to be managed. The smaller the chamber, the higher the compression. If you're building a stroker, compression will increase significantly.

Ford Performance Cylinder Heads

The broadest selection of aftermarket cylinder heads really isn't through the aftermarket at all. Ford Performance (formerly known as Ford Racing and Ford Motorsport Special Vehicle Operations [SVO]) has offered many options for performance enthusiasts. Selection isn't what it used be because Ford Performance is more focused on the Modular and Coyote engines today. Some of these time-proven heads are still available from Ford Performance. Others have been discontinued and are available either used or NOS in their original packaging.

The best part regarding Ford Performance aftermarket heads is the ease of selection along with simplicity. You don't need to search for factory iron castings, such as 289 Hi-Po or 351W heads, anymore. Ford Performance or the used aftermarket has a cylinder head for virtually every application.

The most common Ford aftermarket head is the GT40 High Flow, which is available in iron or aluminum. If you want a more stock appearance that offers a performance improvement, the GT40 is a good cylinder head to choose. The GT40, with good port, bowl, and chamber work, will improve horsepower on the high end due to 1.840/1.540-inch intake/exhaust valves that can easily be grown to 1.940/1.600-inch valves (the Chevrolet intake-valve size). The GT40's 65.5-cc chambers are a nice compromise between older 54- to 55-cc and 70-plus-cc chambers. You can mill this cylinder head's deck surface to reduce the chamber size and raise compression.

The GT40 Turbo-Swirl cylinder head is now known as the "M-6049-X306" and "X307" for 289/302/351W engines. The X306 aluminum head has a 64-cc chamber. The X307 head has a 58-cc chamber. Intake ports flow 240 cfm at 0.550-inch lift. The exhaust flows 170 cfm at 0.500-inch lift. This head is machined for 1.940/1.600-inch intake/exhaust valves. Your pistons must have valve reliefs to reduce the risk of valve-to-piston contact. You must also check intake-manifold port compatibility by doing a gasket match. A nice thing about the GT40 head is that it is compatible with just about any small-block intake manifold or header.

The Z aluminum cylinder head is a great alternative to the Turbo-Swirl for daily driving and weekend racing. Made of A356 T6 cast aluminum, the Z head offers improved flow numbers and more power if you give it your best attention. The Z mandates a competition valve job and bowl work. This is a CNC-ported head that can be purchased from Ford Performance. You get premium stainless-steel 2.020/1.600-inch intake/exhaust valves for more horsepower and improved mid-range torque. Beehive valve springs eliminate valve float. Laser-cut guide plates yield the perfect fit. Expect 319.7-cfm intake flow and 227.7-cfm exhaust flow at 0.550 inch.

The cast-iron Ford Performance Sportsman head (M-6049-N351) is a nice compromise between the Z head, GT40 Turbo-Swirl, and the Yates NASCAR head. It has 2.020/1.600-inch valves for improved flow along with 64-cc chambers. This head is suggested more for 351W engines but can be used on the 289/302 by using a head-bolt adaptor kit. The Sportsman head accepts an M-6569-C351 stud girdle.

The Robert Yates High-Port aluminum head is a NASCAR-level race head (M-6049-C3) with a 40-cc chamber. It comes bare, and you get to choose what goes inside. There's also the M-6049-C3L Yates head with 67-cc chambers for reduced compression. Huge 2.100/1.600-inch intake/exhaust valves occupy both heads. Because this is an all-out race head, it is not suggested for the street. However, it is surely a Ford cylinder head. Because it is a race head, plan to make all kinds of modifications.

Ford Performance Cylinder Head Quick Facts

Head Type	Material	Part Number	Chamber Size	Valve Size (Intake/Exhaust)
GT40 High Flow	Iron	M-6049-L302	65.5 cc	1.840/1.540 inches
GT40 High Flow	Iron	M-6049-L303	65.5 cc	1.840/1.540 inches
GT40 Turbo-Swirl	Aluminum	M-6049-Y303	64 cc	1.940/1.600 inches
GT40 Turbo-Swirl	Aluminum	M-6049-X302	64 cc	1.940/1.600 inches
GT40 Turbo-Swirl	Aluminum	M-6049-X303	58 cc	1.940/1.600 inches
GT40 Turbo-Swirl	Aluminum	M-6049-X304	64 cc	1.940/1.600 inches
GT40 Turbo-Swirl	Aluminum	M-6049-X305	58 cc	1.940/1.600 inches
Turbo-Swirl	Aluminum	M-6049-X306	64 cc	1.940/1.600 inches
Turbo-Swirl	Aluminum	M-6049-X307	58 cc	1.940/1.600 inches
Z Head (Bare)	Aluminum	M-6049-Z304D	63 cc	2.020/1.600 inches
Z Head (Complete)	Aluminum	M-6049-304DA	63 cc	2.020/1.600 inches
Z Head (CNC-ported)	Aluminum	M-6049-Z304P	63 cc	2.020/1.600 inches
Sportsman (Race Only)	Iron	M-6049-N351	64 cc	2.020/1.600 inches
High Port (Race Only)	Aluminum	M-6049-SC1	40–70 cc	2.180/1.620 inches
High Port (NASCAR)	Aluminum	M-6049-D3	N/A	2.180/1.620 inches
High Port (NASCAR—without seats, guides, or pushrod holes)	Aluminum	M-6049-D35	N/A	2.180/1.620 inches

Dart Machinery

In the years since Richard Maskin founded Dart Machinery more than 40 years ago, it has always been about aftermarket cylinder heads, intake manifolds, and engine blocks. Dart is well-known for race-caliber intakes, cylinder heads, and block castings.

Iron Eagle and Pro 1 cylinder heads are engineered and manufactured using state-of-the-art CNC machining centers, a computer-controlled dynamometer, and its own proprietary Speed Flow technology. Iron Eagle cylinder heads for the small-block Ford are basically stock replacement heads with little advantage over stock castings. For what you'd spend on Iron Eagle head castings, you can gain more from the aluminum Pro 1 cylinder heads.

The Pro 1 family of cylinder heads is an excellent street, strip, and oval-track aluminum casting. The base Pro 1 20-degree, 170-cc aluminum heads have high-flow "as-cast" ports with profiled valve-guide bosses, and they are bowl blended on five-axis CNC machining centers. Valve sizing is 1.940/1.600-inch intake/exhaust with a 62-cc chamber. Expect good low- to mid-range torque and throttle response all the way to 6,000 rpm. Valve angle and spacing is retained for compatibility. Exhaust runners are raised 0.135 inch for improved scavenging.

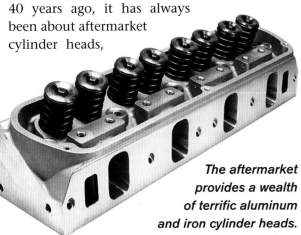

The aftermarket provides a wealth of terrific aluminum and iron cylinder heads. The best choice, of course, is to use aluminum heads, which transfer heat better than iron, reducing the chance of detonation. This enables you to run more aggressive timing along with a leaner mixture. This is the Dart Pro 1 cylinder head.

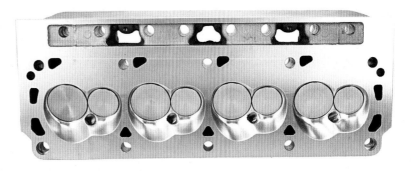

Dart's Pro 1 aluminum cylinder heads cover a wide range of applications because they are designed for both street performance and mild bracket racing, which offers excellent mid-range power. I like these fast-burn chambers, which keep fuel droplets in suspension. Larger 2.020/1.600-inch valves deliver better flow with minimal valve shrouding.

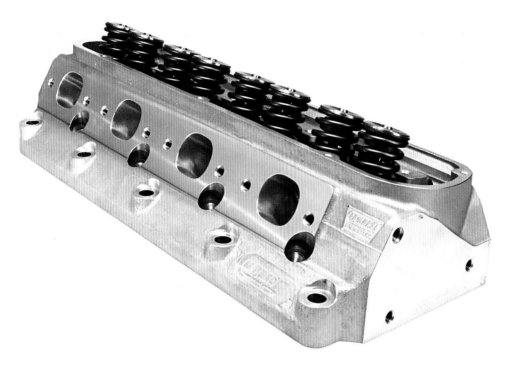

Dart's as-cast ports flow more than most ported designs. Dart offers fully CNC-machined heads with every intake port, exhaust runner, valve bowl, and combustion chamber. The heads are shaped by Dart's five-axis, computer-controlled machining centers, which produce compound curves and complex shapes that no human could duplicate by hand.

Manganese bronze valve guides on all Pro 1 heads deliver durability along with hardened valve seats.

The upscale Pro 1 20-degree 195-cc casting is optimal for the street, mild bracket racing, and oval-track competition with 2.020/1.600-inch intake/exhaust valve sizing with either 58- or 62-cc chambers. Peak torque and throttle response is from idle through 6,800 rpm, and it is best for 347- to 427-ci engines with generous displacement. The Pro 1 195-cc casting offers both 2.500- and 3.000-inch exhaust bolt-hole patterns.

The next-level Dart Pro 1 20-degree, 210-cc head is a terrific street, strip, and oval-track casting with 2.050/1.600-inch intake/exhaust valves and 62-cc chambers. The maximum torque and throttle response is from 3,000 to 7,000-plus rpm. This head is compatible with 347- to 427-ci stroker engines. The Pro 1 210-cc version is a professional-quality competition cylinder head. The Pro 1 210-cc head has both the 2.500- and 3.000-inch exhaust bolt-hole patterns.

The Pro 1 20-degree, 225-cc cylinder head is engineered for real street performance, bracket racing, and oval-track racing with 2.080/1.600-inch valving and 62-cc chambers. Maximum torque and throttle response is from 3,500 to 7,800 rpm. The 225-cc head is best for 363- to 427-ci stroker engines. These heads are optimal for high-compression, big-displacement small-blocks and supercharged applications. This head has a 3.000-inch exhaust bolt-hole pattern.

AFR

The beginnings of Air Flow Research (AFR) date back to 1970 and founder Ken Sperling. AFR was the first company with CNC-ported cylinder heads. This commitment to performance enthusiasts has enabled AFR to find a home in some of the fastest race cars in the world. Its research and development process, along with manufacturing and product testing, are part of the daily operation to search for improvement. AFR manufactures products in Southern California.

AFR's 165-cc Street cylinder head is an affordable choice over reworked factory heads, with 1.900/1.600-inch intake/exhaust valve sizing and 58-cc chambers. These A356 aluminum heads are CNC machined at the intake, exhaust, and chamber. They are ideal for street, towing, or street/strip engines with displacements up to 351 ci that have an operating range from idle to 6,000 rpm. They are street legal via California Air Resources Board (CARB) Executive Order (EO) D-250-3.

The AFR 185-cc Street A356 aluminum cylinder head has CNC-ported intake, exhaust, and chambers with 2.020/1.600-inch intake/exhaust valves and either 58- or 72-cc chambers. The AFR 185-cc head is suitable for 302- to 393-ci applications with a maximum of 6,000 to 6,500 rpm. This head is street legal in 50 states for 1995-and-older emissions-controlled vehicles. It is governed under CARB EO D-250-3 and is not compatible with OEM pistons.

The AFR 195-cc Competition cylinder head has 2.050/1.600-inch intake/exhaust valves with either 58- or 72-cc chambers. It is recommended for displacements up to 408 ci

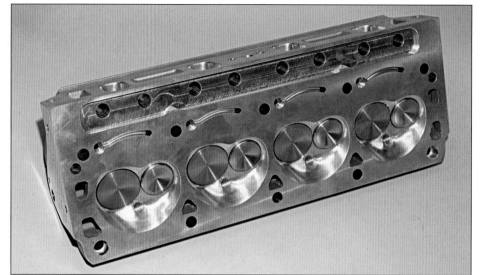

Air Flow Research (AFR) needs little introduction with engine builders and enthusiasts. The company manufactured small-block Ford heads before any other company during the Pro 5.0 movement in the 1990s. Check out these fast-burn chambers with 2.020/1.600-inch valves. These heads consistently deliver incredible numbers.

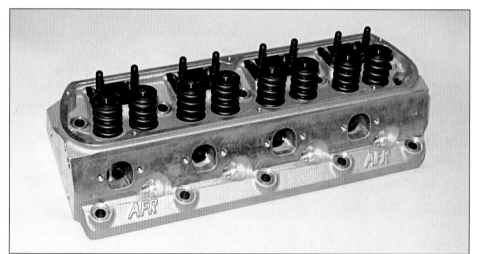

This is one of the early AFR cylinder heads from an engine build that I covered in the 1990s with D-Port exhaust ports. AFR has never produced a bad head based on my experience with AFR castings and reputable engine builders.

The CNC-machined AFR intake ports keep fuel droplets in proper suspension ahead of the valves. This fosters more complete combustion and a good power takeaway.

with an operating range of up to 6,500 to 6,800 rpm. This head is not compatible with OEM pistons nor is it street legal, which depends on the laws in your state. The AFR Competition 205-cc head falls under a similar description, with 2.080/1.600-inch valving and the choice of either 58- or 72-cc chambers. The AFR Competition 220-cc head is fitted with 2.010/1.570-inch valves with either 58- or 72-cc chambers.

Edelbrock

Edelbrock offers the broadest selection of cylinder heads. The

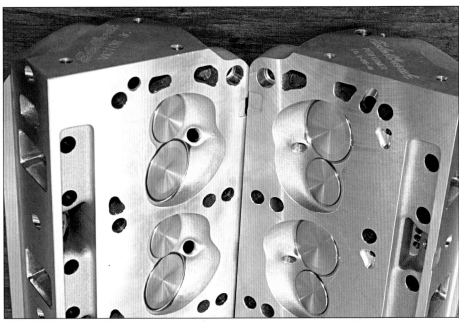

The Victor Jr. (left) and the Performer RPM (right) are placed side by side. The Victor has larger ports for high-RPM operation along with larger 2.050/1.600-inch valve sizing, which is optimal for road racing and the drag strip. The Performer RPM is a terrific street head for daily pavement duty and the weekend getaway.

Edelbrock offers an extensive line of Performer RPM and Victor Jr. cylinder heads for the street and strip. The Performer RPM has the right sizing of ports and valves, which provides good low- to mid-range torque for the street and high RPM for Saturday nights at the drags. The Victor Series is more of a race head, but it can be used for the street.

Modern technology has provided more refined combustion chambers with improved swirl and quench. However, the main thing to watch out for is valve shrouding, which hinders flow.

E-Series and Performer series are affordable street/strip heads for the amateur weekend cruiser and racer. For the more serious performance enthusiast, the Victor Jr. and the Victor/Super Victor castings are offered.

The Edelbrock E-Street cylinder heads offer great engineering and affordable performance with as-cast ports. They are designed for entry-level street-performance applications in the idle-to-5,500-rpm range. E-Street castings are nice bolt-on stock replacement aluminum heads for the 289/302/351W small-block.

The Performer and Performer RPM-series cylinder heads are a step up from the E-Street heads. The Performer and Performer RPM-series heads are excellent street/strip heads for serious weekend drag and road racers. Valve sizing ranges from 1.900/1.600 inches to 2.020/1.600 inches. You may wonder why exhaust valve sizing isn't higher, with 2.020-inch-valve heads. The answer is space and scavenging. You want velocity in an exhaust port for healthy scavenging, depending upon valve overlap.

The Performer head casting is more about street performance with good low- to mid-range torque than horsepower. The Performer RPM is designed more for mid-range to high RPM. Victor Jr. heads are ideal for those who need affordable heads that also make a lot of power. The Victor Jr. head is engineered for competition and extreme performance street engines. Out of the box, it delivers great horsepower and RPM potential at an affordable price. This piece features ductile-iron valve seats and phosphor-bronze guides for the durability that is required in racing. In addition, it's a nice bolt-on swap.

You can have all the valve size in the world but fall short on flow from valve shrouding. Watch the valve sizing and see how it can hinder flow, despite being larger. The chambers can be machined just enough to improve shroud, but you need to watch chamber size and compression.

The Victor Jr. (left) and Performer RPM (right) have the same 60-cc chambers, with the exception of valve sizing. The Victors have 2.050-inch intake valves, whereas the Performer RPMs have 2.020- and 1.900-inch intake valves. Edelbrock makes it easy to choose a head.

The high-end Victor Series Race head is strictly a competition piece with huge 2.150/1.625-inch intake/exhaust valves, and it has the latest induction technology that you want from a race head. The Victor offers beefier rocker stud mounts that can handle the grueling rigors of racing. There's also the Victor/Glidden competition head that has been engineered strictly for racing with 2.240/1.640-inch stopcocks and 24-cc chambers for extreme compression. Visit Edelbrock's website at edelbrock.com for more details.

More affordable and obscure budget heads are available from Summit, Speedway, Jegs, and a host of other retailers that you may consider if your budget is tight and the mainstream castings are out of the running. These heads offer a lot for the price and are worth considering. Look at the specifications and check reviews before purchasing.

Head Work

Basic cylinder-head reconditioning or improving begins with valve function. The intake and exhaust valves allow fuel and air into the chamber and then seal the cylinder for the compression, ignition, and power cycles. Then, the exhaust valves allow the egress of the hot gasses. To fully contain the heat energy, the valves must close quickly and open in proper time with the piston and crankshaft events. Ideally, valve overlap allows for the swift exit of the hot gasses as the intake valve opens to allow for a quick entrance of air and fuel.

A simple valve job involves disassembly; cleaning the castings; examining the valves, guides, and seats; determining the condition of the

Port size is determined by how the engine is intended to be used. You can have too much intake port and lose low- to mid-range torque on the street. This is an aftermarket Cleveland head that has been adapted for the small-block Ford with 351C-2V-sized intake ports, such as the Aussie head, which is a nice compromise.

This is the exhaust side of the aftermarket Cleveland head, and it is a nice compromise regarding the size to allow for good scavenging.

parts; and either replacing or returning the parts. It is always best to replace the valves, springs, keepers, retainers, and guides even if you have parts in good working condition.

The exhaust valves are the hottest parts in an engine. If you have iron heads that were manufactured prior to 1972, you will need hardened exhaust-valve seats. One affordable option is to use stainless-steel valves that won't wear down or damage the iron valve seat. It is also important to consider the valve-seat angle and what it can add or take away from flow and performance. A basic three-angle valve job is the most common, but you will sacrifice performance from limited flow. A multi-angle valve job improves flow around the valve and seat. Seasoned engine builders have said that you want sufficient seat contact for valve cooling with a smooth, unobstructed relationship between the valve and seat.

Another important issue is regarding valve guides. You can ream the guides and install bronze bushings (liners) that will perform quite well and control oil flow to the valve stems. You may also replace the valve guides with steel guides, and they will be good for a long time to come.

Not enough thought is given to valve-head shape, which also affects power. Be mindful of materials that maintain durability. Valve weight is very important to ensure effective high-RPM operation along with valve-head shape. You want a sufficient contact surface for cooling. At the same time, you want a multi-angle valve job for improved flow.

This is a typical flow bench that is used for cylinder-head-port flow testing. These are test valve springs that are used to hold the valves at various lifts during testing. The valves are held open at lifts ranging from 0.100-to 0.600-inch lift, with flow numbers being recorded with each lift number.

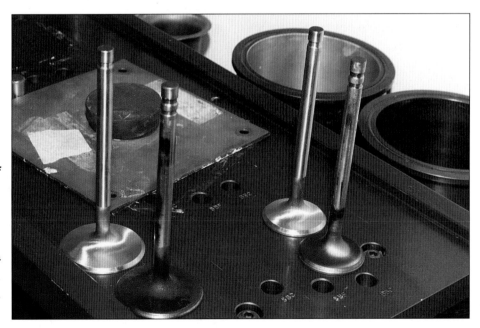

CAMSHAFT AND VALVETRAIN

Camshaft and valvetrain selection are the most important segments of a small-block build. This stage of a build determines not only the engine's behavior but also how reliably and predictably the engine will perform. To understand how to select a camshaft and valvetrain for your engine, you must first understand how a camshaft and the valvetrain works and how to select components.

Selecting the right camshaft profile comes from how you want an engine to perform. Are you building a daily driver where low- and mid-range torque are important or are you building a high-revving racing engine that makes its peak torque at high RPM? A camshaft manufacturer's catalog lists dozens of camshaft profiles for the same type of engine. This is where it gets confusing for the novice. Terms such as lift, duration, lobe separation, base circle, lobe centerline angle, and valve over-

Flat tappets don't sit squarely on the cam lobe. They sit to one side in order to spin as they ride the cam lobe, which reduces resistance and distributes wear.

From 1962–1966, the small-block Ford valvetrain used what is shown (conventional cast rocker arms and a flat-tappet camshaft). Most 221/260/289 engines had hydraulic flat tappets and three-piece pushrods. The 289 High Performance V-8, which was introduced in 1963 and produced through 1967, sported an aggressive flat-tappet mechanical cam, which delivered peak torque and horsepower at 6,000 rpm.

Aggressive camshafts really hammer the valve springs. These dampers inside the valve spring provide stability and cooling.

A roller cam (left) and a flat-tappet cam (right) are shown side by side. Although the roller-tappet cam approach is nothing new, it is a better idea because it enables a more aggressive profile without sacrificing idle and drive quality. The roller cam also reduces internal friction, which frees up power.

lap must be understood. What does this information mean, and how will it affect your engine's performance and durability?

Camshaft Function

A camshaft's profile includes the lobe design, dimension, positioning, when it opens the valve, when the valve closes, how long it will keep the valve open, and how far it opens the valve. These are the dimensions of a cam profile.

Flat-tappet camshafts work differently than roller camshafts. In fact, flat-tappet camshafts don't make much sense anymore unless you are on a very limited budget. Flat-tappet camshafts limit what can be done with the lobe profile. If you want an aggressive profile (a hot

Cam Speak

- *Lift* is the maximum amount that a valve-lifter-pushrod combination can be raised off the base circle. Lift is measured in thousands of an inch (0.001 inch) typically from 0.100 to 0.700 inch. The lobe profile determines how quickly this occurs. It can be smooth or abrupt, depending on the lobe profile.
- *Duration* is the amount of time that the valve is open, beginning when the valve unseats. By this, I mean the number of degrees that the camshaft will rotate when cam lift begins. Duration typically begins at 0.004 inch of cam lift or when the lifter begins to ride the ramp coming off the base circle. "Duration at 50" means a duration measurement begins at 0.050 inch of cam lift. Duration at 50 is the industry standard for determining camshaft lobe duration. When reading camshaft specifications, duration at 50 is the specification that you will normally see.
- *Lobe separation* (also known as lobe center) is the distance (in degrees) between the intake-lobe peak lift and the exhaust-lobe peak lift. Lobe separation generally runs between 102 and 114 degrees (camshaft degrees).
- The *intake centerline* is the position of the camshaft in relation to the crankshaft. For example, an intake centerline of 114 degrees means that the intake valve reaches maximum lift at 114 degrees after top dead center (ATDC).
- The *exhaust centerline* is basically the same thing as the intake centerline. It is when the exhaust valve reaches maximum lift before top dead center (BTDC) in degrees.
- *Valve verlap* is when both the intake and exhaust valves are off their seats to allow for proper cylinder scavenging. Overlap occurs when the exhaust valve is closing and the piston is reaching TDC. The intake charge from the opening intake valve pushes the exhaust gasses out.
- *Adjustable valve timing* is being able to dial in a camshaft by adjusting valve timing at the timing sprocket. By adjusting the valve timing at the sprocket, you can increase or decrease torque. If the valve timing is advanced, torque is increased but horsepower is lost. If the valve timing is retarded, torque is decreased but horsepower is gained. It's a compromise. ■

All engine-build plans should include matched components that have been engineered to work together. These are T&D-matched valvetrain components: shaft-mounted rockers, mechanical tappets, an aggressive Comp roller cam, and one-piece pushrods. Never compromise on components that can make or break an engine build.

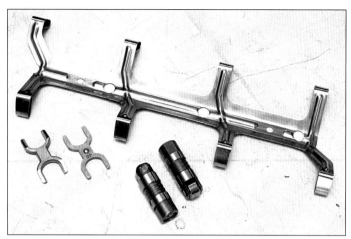

Beginning in 1985, 5.0L High Output engines received a new heavy-duty roller block that was designed to accom-modate a roller-tappet camshaft, which made a huge dif-ference in performance. The hydraulic roller tappets were secured with this "spider" that secured to the lifter valley. Non-roller blocks may also be fitted with roller tappets and the spider system or linked roller lifters.

Unlike flat tappets, roller lifters are lubricated exclusively with engine assembly lube at the roller and never molyb-denum (moly lube) grease. Flat tappets get molybdenum at the lifter face and at the cam lobe for hard hardening during break-in.

The camshaft installation procedure is different for roller and flat-tappet cams. Flat-tappet cams get molybdenum grease (moly lube) on their hardened faces against the cam lobe. Moly lube is critical to proper flat-tappet cam break-in.

Lift, duration, lobe separation angle, valve overlap, and base circle are all camshaft elements. They determine valve timing events and function. (Image Courtesy Comp Cams)

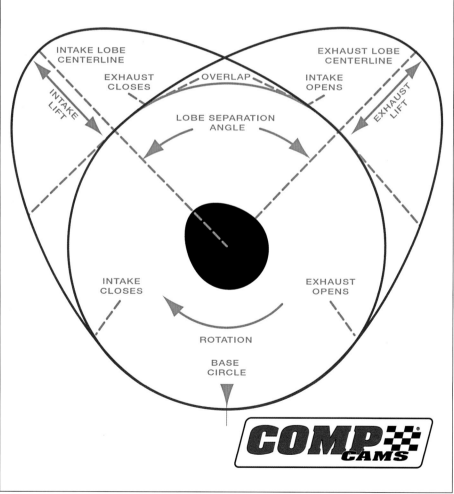

Exhaust Valve Open

This is where valve function becomes more involved. There's cam-lobe lift and there's also valve lift. Lobe lift, for example, is 0.280 inch at the lobes. The ratio of the rocker arm on top (a 1.6:1 ratio) is multiplied by the lobe lift to determine the valve lift. A 0.280-inch lobe lift with a 1.6:1 rocker-arm ratio has a 0.448-inch valve lift. (Photo Courtesy Comp Cams)

cam) with flat tappets, you can only go so far or you will suffer poor drivability (rough idle and low manifold vacuum).

Roller cams cost considerably more than flat-tappet cams. However, they're worth every penny in terms of performance and durability. You can run a more aggressive cam profile and get away with it with a roller cam.

Street Camshafts

The best street-performance cams are ground with a lobe separation angle (LSA) of between 108 and 114 degrees. When the LSA is around 112 degrees, drivability is improved because the engine idles smoother and makes better low-end torque. There's also more vacuum at idle for accessories, such as power brakes and climate control. Any time that the LSA is below 108 degrees, idle qual-

ity and streetability suffer. However, there's more to it than just the LSA.

Compression and valve timing must be considered together because one affects the other. Valve-timing events directly affect cylinder pressure and ultimately the working/dynamic compression. Long intake-valve duration reduces cylinder pressure. Shorter intake duration increases cylinder pressure. Too much cylinder pressure can cause detonation (pinging). Too little cylinder pressure results in a decrease of torque. You can count on cam manufacturers to figure stock compression ratios into their camshaft-selection tables, which makes selecting a camshaft easier than it's ever been. Plug your application into the equation, and you will be pleased with the result most of the time.

Be conservative with your camshaft specifications if you want reliability and an engine that will live a

long time. Stay with a conservative lift profile (0.500-inch lift). High-lift camshafts are hard on the valvetrain. They put valve-to-piston clearances at risk. Watch duration and lobe separation closely, which will help you be more effective in camshaft selection. Instead of opening the valve more (lift), you want to open it longer (duration) and in better efficiency with piston timing (overlap or lobe separation).

Always keep in mind the parts that you will use for induction, cylinder heads, and exhaust. Savvy engine architects understand that to work effectively, an engine must have matched components. The cam, valvetrain, heads, intake manifold, and exhaust system must all work as a team. When using stock cylinder heads, the cam profile should not be too aggressive. Opt for a cam profile that will provide good low- to mid-range torque. Torque doesn't do you any good on the street when it happens at 6,000 rpm. Select a cam profile that will make good torque between 2,500 and 4,500 rpm.

Note how the cam will work with your cylinder heads. Some camshafts actually lose power with a given head because there's too much lift or duration. This is why researching a cylinder head before selecting a camshaft is important.

What type of fuel do you intend to run? This also affects camshaft selection. You can raise the compression if you're running a mild camshaft profile or using a higher-octane fuel. Camshaft timing events must be directly tied to the compression ratio. The longer the duration, the lower the cylinder pressure and working compression are. The shorter the duration, less air will be allowed into the cylinder, which also affects working compression. The objective needs to be the highest compression that is possible without detonation. Aim for the most duration possible without compression extremes.

Valve overlap, as stated earlier, is the period between the exhaust stroke and intake stroke when both valves are off their seats. This improves exhaust scavenging and cylinder filling. It improves exhaust scavenging by allowing the incoming intake charge to push the remaining exhaust gasses out via the closing exhaust valve. If the exhaust valve completely closed, there wouldn't be any scavenging. The greater the overlap in a street engine, the less torque the engine will make down low, where it is needed the most.

Street engines need 10 to 55 degrees of valve overlap to be effective in making torque. When valve overlap starts going beyond 55 degrees, the torque down low falters. A powerful street engine will need greater than 55 degrees of valve overlap—but not much greater. To provide an idea of what I'm talking about, racing engines need 70 to 115 degrees of valve overlap because that is what is needed at high RPM.

LSA is another area of consideration in street cam selection. This cam dynamic is chosen based on displacement and how the engine will be used. Consider lobe separation based on how much displacement and valve size that you are using. The smaller the valves, the tighter (fewer degrees) that the lobe separation should be. However, tighter lobe separation does adversely affect idle quality. Therefore, most camshaft manufacturers spec their cams with wider LSAs than the custom grinders.

Duration in a street engine is the most important dynamic to consider in the cam selection process. Duration is increased whenever less lift is desired. Why? Because airflow goes into the cylinder bore in two ways: lift and duration. The valve can be opened more often and for less time to get airflow. The valve can also be opened fewer times with a longer duration to get airflow. Each way has a different effect on performance. Duration is determined by how much cylinder head and displacement you have, and how the engine will be used. Excessive duration hurts low-end torque, which is what is needed on the street.

Balance is achieved by maximizing duration without a loss in low-end torque. This is done by using the right heads with proper valve sizing. Large valves and ports do not work well for street use because velocity and torque are lacking. The smaller the ports and valves, the greater the velocity and corresponding torque.

What does this say about duration? You want greater duration whenever displacement and valve size increases. Increasing duration falls directly in line with torque peak and RPM range. This does not mean that any torque is necessarily gained as RPM increases. It means that peak torque comes in at a higher RPM range. For example, if the engine is making 350 ft-lbs of torque at 4,500 rpm, and you increase duration, peak torque will come in at a higher RPM range.

Compression has a direct effect on what the duration should be. When running higher compression, watch the duration closely because it can drive up cylinder pressures. Sometimes you can curb compression and run greater duration, depending on how you want to make power. When you have greater duration, the engine is going to make more power on the high end and less on the low end.

Higher compression with a shorter duration helps the engine make low-end torque where it is needed most on the street. The things to watch for with compression are detonation and overheating. Detonation can do significant engine damage when you're at wide-open throttle. Maximum street compression should be 10.0:1, depending on the cylinder head and cam that you've selected.

Valve lift is an issue that you must think about as it pertains to an engine's needs. For example, small-block engines generally need more valve lift than big-block engines. As lift is increased, torque is generally increased. This is especially important at low- and mid-range RPM, where it happens most on the street. Your objective needs to be more torque with less RPM if you want your engine to live longer. Revs drain the life out of an engine.

To make good low-end torque with a small-block Ford, a camshaft that will offer a combination of effective lift and duration is needed. Run longer intake duration to make the most of valve lift. You get valve lift via cam lobes to be sure. However, the rocker-arm ratio is the other half of the lift equation. The most common rocker-arm ratio is 1.6:1, which means that the rocker arm will give the valve 1.6 times the lift that is at the cam lobe. When you go with a 1.7:1-ratio rocker arm, valve lift becomes 1.7 times what is found at the lobe.

It is best to spec a cam on the side of conservatism, especially when building an engine for daily use and weekend bracket racing. When opting for an aggressive camshaft with a lot of lift, you're putting more stress on the valve stems, valve guides, and valve springs. The constant hammering of daily use with excessive lift is what makes engines fail.

Dual-Pattern Camshafts

A dual-pattern camshaft runs different lobe profiles on the intake and exhaust side to meet specific performance needs. A single-pattern cam provides excellent low-end torque, and now that the market has many options for great-flowing heads and exhaust systems, the benefits of a dual-pattern cam has been largely negated.

It is beneficial to use a dual-pattern cam whenever you run nitrous oxide, a supercharger, or a turbocharger, where exhaust scavenging is rapid and furious. Running a dual-pattern camshaft on the street with good-flowing heads and exhaust doesn't make much sense because you will lose torque and fuel economy in the low- and mid-RPM ranges. Keeping the exhaust valve open longer helps a street engine make power, which is why, when you look at specs for dual-pattern cams, the duration on the exhaust lobe is usually 10 degrees greater. This is especially important with small-block Fords, which suffer from restrictive exhaust ports that call for greater lift and/or duration on the exhaust side.

Racing Camshafts

When building an engine for racing, it is a different picture than is found with street engines. Camshaft profile in a racing engine depends upon the type of racing, vehicle

Utter confusion abounds with cam thrust plates and small-block Fords. Early 221/260/289 engines prior to 1965 have this two-piece thrust plate with countersunk screws and a "C" spacer between the cam and sprocket.

These are the two basic small-block Ford cam sprockets. The early pre-1965 sprocket (left) goes with the two-piece cam thrust plate. Above it is the "C" spacer that goes with the early sprocket.

weight and type, the type of transmission, and the rear axle ratio.

Drag racing mandates a different camshaft profile than road or circle-track racing. For example, a

This is the more common cam thrust plate that was used on small-block Fords with an oil gallery from the cam journal to the distributor drive gear. Some plates have this gallery channel, while others do not. This cam plate can be adapted to earlier small-blocks when using a compatible camshaft and related hardware.

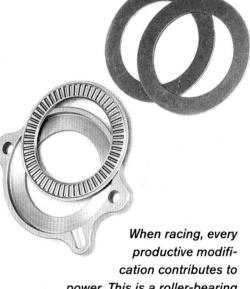

When racing, every productive modification contributes to power. This is a roller-bearing cam thrust plate, which reduces internal friction and frees up power.

short-track racing engine must be able to produce huge amounts of torque in short order. The same is true for a drag racer. These issues teach us something about engine breathing. Breathing effectiveness is determined by the camshaft profile.

The lobe separation for a drag-racing camshaft is between 104 and 118 degrees, which is a broad range because drag-racing needs can vary substantially. This is where you have to custom dial in your application with a camshaft grinder. Most camshaft grinders have computation charts that show the right cam for your application. As your needs change, so must the camshaft profile.

When road racing, lobe separation should be in the 106-degree range because you want peak torque to come on sooner. The downside is that torque tends to fall off a cliff quickly. Some cam grinders push lobe separation higher for circle-track engines, which depends upon track condition and length.

Generally, the higher the lobe separation, the broader the torque curve (more torque over a broader RPM range). An oval-track small-block engine needs good low- to mid-range torque to come out of the turns more aggressively, which calls for higher lobe separation. A wider lobe separation smooths out the idle and yields a broader torque curve.

Why Degree a Camshaft?

Making power isn't just about adding displacement, large-port heads, a big carburetor, and a lumpy camshaft. It is about the physics of packaging and tuning your engine properly. So, why do we degree camshafts after they're installed in an engine?

The most basic reason for degreeing a camshaft is to confirm that you have the correct grind for the job and that your cam matches the card. Camshaft grinders today employ the most advanced technology that is available. As a result, very few faulty camshafts ever make it to the consumer. However, camshafts get mis-

Cam degreeing proves the cam specifications. Rarely do actual numbers match the manufacturer's cam card. However, they need to come close.

packaged and improperly ground at times, which means that you could receive a completely different grind than the cam card and packaging state. This is why you should fact-check during cam installation.

When degreeing a camshaft, determine the valve timing events as they relate to the crankshaft position. The crankshaft makes 2 complete revolutions for every 1 revolution of the camshaft. One full revolution of each is 360 degrees. This means that the crank turns 720 degrees and the cam turns 360 degrees. Think of rotation like a pie. Half of a turn is 180 degrees. A quarter of a turn is 90 degrees.

Duration is the number of degrees of rotation that the camshaft will make from the time that the valve begins to open until the time it closes. When there is 244 degrees of duration, this means that there is 244 degrees of camshaft rotation from valve unseat to valve seat. Overlap or lobe separation is the number of degrees between maximum-valve-lift intake and maximum-valve-lift exhaust. With all of this in mind, you can degree the camshaft timing events in time with piston travel.

Degree a camshaft by bolting a degree wheel to the crankshaft,

Stock and mild performance builds do not need a roller chain, although the roller chain reduces internal friction. A stock chain is adequate for most street applications.

cranking the number-1 piston to top dead center (TDC), finding true TDC, and installing a timing pointer. You can purchase a degree wheel kit (part number SUM-G-1057 from Summit Racing).

I find TDC with a bolt-on piston stop that bolts to the deck or screws into the spark-plug hole. I suggest doing this with the cylinder head removed to provide the greatest accuracy because you want true TDC. Begin this process by turning the crankshaft clockwise until the

A dual-roller chain improves accuracy and reduces internal friction via the use of dual rollers in the chain. Rollers function with greatly reduced friction because they roll (instead of riding over one another with resistance like the teeth in a conventional chain).

When installing a dual-roller chain, remove the factory oil slinger, which is there to keep oil away from the crank seal and to sling lubrication around the timing components. The oil slinger can interfere with the dual-roller chain, resulting in engine damage.

number-1 piston comes up to TDC and you are smack in the middle of crank rollover with the rod at 12 o'clock. With the cylinder head installed, hold your thumb over the spark-plug hole and listen to the air being forced out by the piston.

At this point, both timing marks on the crank and camshaft sprockets should be in perfect alignment at 12 and 6 o'clock. Install the degree wheel next and align the bolt-on timing pointer. With all of this accomplished, the number-1 piston should be at TDC, with the degree wheel and pointer at 0 degrees. This is what's known as true TDC, and it becomes the base point of reference. Everything from here on out becomes before top dead center (BTDC) or after top dead center (ATDC). The intake valve will open at a given number of degrees ATDC and close at a given number of degrees BTDC. The exhaust valve will open at a given number of degrees BTDC and close at a given number of degrees ATDC. Much of this depends upon valve overlap.

Timing Components

The aftermarket offers a wide variety of timing sets and belt drives for small-block Fords. The choice tends to be simple, depending on the type of engine that you want to build. If you're building a stocker, a standard OEM-style set is all that you need. A dual-roller timing set reduces friction and makes valve timing crispy. You can run a dual roller with a stock engine. These wear better and reduce internal friction. If you're concerned about valve timing, opt for an adjustable timing set with an adjustable crank sprocket. There are also adjustable-cam-sprocket timing

sets from a wide variety of sources.

An option for avid racers is a belt drive. Belt drives generate less friction, effectively damp adverse harmonics before they reach the valvetrain, maintain precision valve timing (particularly at high engine speeds), and are convenient when it comes to fast turnaround valve timing adjustments.

An adjustable drive-belt idler is included on the Innovators West drive belt for precise adjustment of drive-belt tension. This is very important when taking into consideration the production tolerances of new belts and the re-tensioning of used belts. A cam retaining plate is provided with two encased roller bearings: one between the camshaft and plate and the other between the cam pulley and plate. Optional high-vacuum seals, an alloy steel drive hub, and a camshaft-drive adapter are available.

Lifters

Four basic lifter (tappet) types are used in small-block Ford engines: 1) flat-tappet hydraulic, 2) flat-tappet mechanical, 3) roller hydraulic, and 4) roller mechanical. Flat-tappet cams were factory installed in 1962–1984 small-block Fords. Roller tappets were used more and more in Ford factory V-8 engines beginning in 1985, which is when the aftermarket got involved. More engine builds are witnessing the use of roller tappets because there's less friction, smoother operation, and the ability to run a more aggressive profile without the drawbacks of a radical flat-tappet camshaft.

Roller tappets are more costly than flat tappets due to tighter tolerances and a greater number of parts.

Their cost puts them outside of the budget-engine category, but they're worth every penny in what they save in wear and tear. They also give you an advantage if your desire is to run a more aggressive camshaft profile.

Although hydraulic lifters had more widespread use beginning in the 1960s, their innovation dates back to the 1920s. Hydraulic lifters don't require periodic adjustment like a mechanical or solid lifter. As the camshaft and valvetrain wear, hydraulic lifters expand with the wear via oil pressure to take up clearance. This keeps operation quiet and reliability sound.

Lifter and cam lobe wear and failure are rarely caused by manufacturing defects. They fail because we don't give them a good start when it's time to fire the engine in the first place. Flat-tappet camshafts must be broken in properly; otherwise, failure is inevitable. Molybdenum lube must be applied to the cam lobe and lifter face. The engine must then be operated at 2,500 rpm for 20 to 30 minutes after the initial fire-up to properly wear in the lobes. Also, use a zinc dialkyldithiophosphate (ZDDP) additive in the oil for a proper break-in.

Roller tappets don't require break-in because rollers and cam lobes enjoy a good low-friction relationship to begin with. Flat-tappet mechanical camshafts are good for high-revving engines, where the inaccuracies of hydraulic camshafts (lifter collapse) are unacceptable. Mechanical camshafts provide accuracy because there's nothing left to chance. Lift moves with the cam lobe with solid precision. Given proper valve lash adjustment, mechanical lifters do the job very well. The thing is that mechanical flat and roller tap-

pets have to be adjusted periodically, which can be annoying on a daily driven street engine. This is where you will need to do some soul searching before selecting a camshaft.

Pushrods and Rocker Arms

Pushrods and rocker arms transfer the cam lobe's energy to the valve stem. Think of the rocker arm as the camshaft's messenger because the rocker arm multiplies lift, which makes the valve open farther than the camshaft's lobe lift. Rocker-arm types range from stock cast affairs all the way to extruded and forged pieces with roller bearings and tips. Forged or extruded roller-rocker arms are quite costly, which generally leaves them out of a budget engine

program. However, this doesn't mean that you must settle for stock cast or stamped-steel pieces, either.

Stock cast or stamped-steel rocker arms don't perform well under the heavy demands of radical camshaft profiles. An aggressive camshaft profile can break a stock rocker arm. This is why it is always best to err on the side of heavy-duty whenever you build an engine. Stamped-steel, ball-stud, roller-tip rocker arms are a good first step toward valvetrain durability whenever you opt for an aggressive camshaft. The roller tip reduces the stress that is experienced with stock rocker arms. The thing is that when lift and valve-spring pressures increase, a stamped-steel or cast roller-tip rocker arm doesn't always stand up to the test, especially when

The more conventional rocker arm on the left was used from 1962 to May 7, 1966, when Ford eliminated the cast-in pushrod guides in the cylinder head. Beginning on May 8, 1966, Ford went to a rail-style rocker arm (right) with longer valve stems. Make sure that the valve stems and rocker arms match. Using a rail-style rocker arm with the short valve stem will lead to engine failure.

Comp Cams offers an affordable roller-tip stamped-steel rocker that reduces internal friction. For the non-rail style (from 1961 to 1967), order Comp Cams part number 1442-1. For the rail style (from 1968–onward), order part number 1431-1, which is available direct from Comp Cams or through Summit Racing. (Photo Courtesy Summit Racing)

These are the classic Comp Pro Magnum roller rocker arms, which are available both used and in remaining speed shop inventories. (Photo Courtesy Comp Cams)

The Ultra Pro Magnum rocker arm from Comp replaced the Pro Magnum roller rocker arm and is a stronger piece.

Valvetrain geometry is important when it comes to durability and performance. The rocker-arm tip must be centered on the valve stem throughout the valve's travel. Otherwise, you risk ruining the valve stem and guide.

Proper valvetrain geometry comes from getting proper push-rod length. If the pushrod length is too short, the rocker-arm tip rides the back of the valve stem. If the pushrod length is too long, it centers too far forward on the valve stem. The tip must be centered on the valve stem.

spring pressures climb to over 350 pounds. Even the best stamped-steel, roller-tip rocker arm will fail when it is overstressed.

When lift and spring pressures go skyward, you're going to want a roller-pivot, roller-tip forged rocker arm for your budget engine build. Going that extra mile with a super-durable rocker arm ensures longer engine life, especially for a daily driver. For a weekend racer, stepping up to a better rocker arm

is like writing a life-insurance policy because marginal rocker arms will not stand up to the high-revving task. Roller-pivot, roller-tip rocker arms also ensure valvetrain precision and accuracy when the revs get high.

Look to Crane Cams, Comp Cams, or Ford Performance for rocker arms and pushrods. These companies all have a lot of valuable experience with valvetrain components and offer a wide selection. A good rule of thumb is to run the same brand of

Use a push-rod checker to get the valvetrain geometry correct. Figure out the proper length, measure the checker, and order your pushrods.

rocker arm and camshaft. See your favorite camshaft company or speed shop for more details.

When it comes to valvetrain adjustment, small-block Ford engines have flexibility in adjustable aftermarket studs where adjustable studs were not originally used. Beginning in 1968, small-block Ford engines received no-adjust, positive-stop rocker-arm studs that are undesirable for the performance buff. From the mid-1970s forward, the rocker-arm stud was replaced with a new-design stamped-steel rocker arm, fulcrum, and bolt that mount atop a boss similar to what the small-block Fords have had in the years since. You can take more current small-block Ford heads and convert them from bolt/fulcrum to adjustable stud.

Valve-Spring Pressures

The installed height of a valve spring is the total height of the spring when the valve is seated. Valve-spring height is measured from where the spring meets the bottom of the retainer to where it seats against the cylinder head. Virtually all camshafts come packaged with recommended valve-spring height information. If you follow the recommended spring height, you will not have a spring that is too weak (causing the valves to float at high RPM) or one that has too much spring pressure.

Valve-seat pressure is the force that the valve spring places on the valve head/face when it is closed. Open-spring pressure is the pressure that forces the valve to close after the rocker arm opens the valve. Open pressure is greater than seat pressure because the spring is under pressure from the cam lobe and rocker arm.

The valve-spring height is being checked here.

Valve-spring pressure is contingent upon the cam profile and revs expected. Aggressive cams need greater valve-spring pressure to snap the valves shut at high RPM.

Valve-spring cups keep the spring centered at high revs. This is a Boss 302 head, which has good valve-spring stability via the cup. Valve-spring cups can be purchased for any small-block Ford build.

Valve-spring shims are added to control the spring height and pressure to keep the spring characteristics the same. However, this also keeps the seat pressure that is lost from either cutting the valve seat or from wear during regular use.

Seat pressure for non-roller hydraulic cams should be around 300 pounds maximum, with 350 pounds for non-roller, flat-tappet mechanical cams. Seat pressure should be roughly 110 to 120 pounds maximum, with flat-tappet mechanical cams at 140 pounds. Roller cams are decidedly different.

Because a roller cam moves the valves at higher velocities, this calls for a spring with more seat pressure, which prevents valve float at high RPM. Also, roller cams don't have the friction that is associated with flat-tappet cams and lifters. As a result, valve springs with higher open pressures (around 500 to 800 pounds at peak valve lift) allow the engine to rev higher.

Spring Height

Always order camshafts in kit form. I suggest following the manufacturer's specifications. If you use matched springs, if you use different springs, or if you change the springs, the spring height must always be checked.

Use a precision rule to measure the spring from where it meets the retainer to where it sits on the cylinder head around the valve guide. Check the installed height without shims installed. More precise than a ruler, a micrometer can fit in place of the valve spring. Turn the dial until

Using shaft-mounted rockers is labor intensive but important to engine life. The T&D rocker installation begins with mounts or pedestals (as shown).

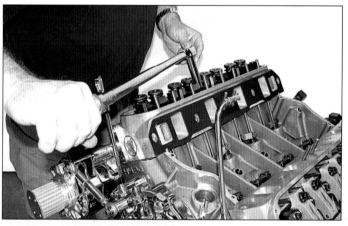

Secure the mounts with a torque wrench and tighten them to the manufacturer's specifications. These mounts are bolted to where a rocker-arm stud would normally be located.

Valvetrain selection depends on how the engine is intended to be used. The Jesel valvetrain components shown here are high-end pieces for competition. The shaft-mounted rockers are used instead of the stud-mounted rockers that would normally be used.

Shaft-mounted rocker arms are mounted next. This is a bulletproof valvetrain system that can take the revs.

Valve lash adjustment is an easy step with these shaft-mounted rockers. Set the lash and lock it in.

Use putty in the valve reliefs to check the valve-to-piston clearances. Temporarily install the head and valvetrain to operate the valves throughout their entire travel. The valves leave an impression in the putty, which provides a good idea of how much room there is. You want a minimum clearance of 0.060 inch.

the valve is seated snug on its seat. Then, note the measurement on the micrometer. If the valve spring is not at the recommended installed height, either shim the spring until it reaches the correct height or machine the spring seat in the head deeper to achieve the installed height that is needed.

Valvetrain Geometry

First, it is important to confirm proper valvetrain geometry, which is the centering of the rocker-arm tip on the valve-stem tip when you're doing valvetrain setup. This happens by using the correct-length pushrod for your application. Purchase a pushrod checker at your favorite speed shop if you're ever in doubt and use it to configure your small-block's rocker-arm tip-to-stem geometry.

A pushrod checker is little more than an adjustable pushrod that can be used to confirm rocker-arm geometry. If the pushrod is too long, the tip will be under-centered on the valve stem, causing excessive side loads toward the outside of the cylinder head. If the pushrod is too short, the rocker-arm tip will be over-centered, causing excessive side loading toward the inside of the head. In either case, side loads on the valve stem and guide cause excessive wear and early failure. This is why the rocker-arm tip should be properly centered on the valve stem for smooth operation.

An accessory that reduces valve-stem-tip wear and side loading is the roller-tip rocker arm. Roller-tip rocker arms roll smoothly across the valve-stem tip, virtually eliminating wear because there's little internal friction. Stamped-steel, roller-tip rocker arms are available at budget prices without the high cost of extruded or forged pieces.

Rocker-Arm Adjustment

If you're building a bolt-fulcrum-rocker-equipped 5.0L or 5.8L engine, there is no valve lash adjustment. The same approach applies to positive-stop, no-adjust rocker arms prior to the late 1970s. Tighten the fulcrum or positive-stop adjustment to the proper torque specifications, and that's the end of it.

If there are valve lash issues with a bolt-fulcrum or positive-stop rocker pivot, the adjustment sometimes calls for pushrods of varying lengths to get the lash into proper adjustment. If you have a noisy rocker arm, confirm the lifter status before doing anything else. A collapsed lifter will cause excessive rocker-arm noise due to excessive lash. Ford says to allow 5 to 55 seconds of lifter leakdown time. A damaged or excessively worn rocker arm will make noise. So will a damaged or excessively worn fulcrum. Ford suggests a 0.060-inch-longer pushrod to help take up excessive clearance. Again, use a pushrod checker.

Many owners will opt for an adjustable stud-mounted rocker

Check the valve lash prior to fire-up. First, check lash cold. Then, check it hot after the first shutdown. Clearances are greater when cold and tighter when hot.

arm with mechanical or hydraulic tappets. There's endless discussion about how to adjust valve lash with hydraulic-lifter engines with stud-mounted rocker arms. Hydraulic-lifter plungers have a very limited amount of travel or preload (0.020 to 0.060 inch at the most). On top, that means approximately a 1/4 to 3/4 turn at the rocker-arm adjustment.

Everyone has his or her own approach to valve lash adjustment with hydraulic lifters. Here's one approach that I picked up from a prominent California engine builder. Begin with the first cylinder on each bank and work your way aft one cylinder at a time. This way, you won't miss any. Valve adjustment is best taken one cylinder at a time with the cam lobe on the base circle

of the valve that you are adjusting. Twirl the pushrod with your fingertips while slowly tightening the rocker-arm-adjustment nut. When the pushrod becomes slightly resistant to turn with your fingertips, you are at zero valve lash, and the lifter is not compressed.

When the intake valve is almost closed, adjust the exhaust-valve lash. When the exhaust valve begins to open, adjust the intake-valve lash. This ensures that the valve you are adjusting is fully closed and you are on the base circle of the cam lobe. How you intend to use the engine determines valve lash. High-revving engines should get zero lash or a 1/8 to 1/4 turn once you hit zero lash. This allows room should the lifter pump up at high RPM. Daily drivers and weekend cruisers can go as much as a half turn. My personal approach is to have valve lash at no more than 1/4 turn. I have also seen engines that will tolerate only zero valve lash—anything more and you will experience misfire and roughness because the valve (or valves) are not seating.

You won't know if you've been successful at valve-lash adjustment until you fire the engine and it's at operating temperature. If there's significant rocker-arm chatter, there's excessive lash. If there's roughness, the valve lash is too tight. Some aftermarket rocker arms, such as the

Hydraulic-lifter valve-lash adjustment is straightforward. With the lifter foot on the cam base circle, slowly run the rocker-arm adjustment down until you start to feel resistance while rotating the pushrod with your fingertips. Tighten the nut 1/8 to 1/4 turn. Lock the nut down. After that first run, check the valve lash again.

Checking camshaft endplay is just as critical as checking crankshaft endplay. Acceptable camshaft endplay is 0.004 to 0.008 inch using a dial indicator at the camshaft sprocket bolt head, sprocket, or fuel-pump eccentric.

Select an adjustable timing set that enables you to advance or retard valve timing. This can be done at the crank or with an adjustable cam sprocket.

Comp Cams Pro Magnum or Ultra Pro Magnum, make a soft clicking sound that is on a par with what you would hear with mechanical tappets, which makes a small-block Ford sound more like it has mechanical tappets. However, it is of no consequence.

Proper valve adjustment is crucial to both performance and durability. A valve that doesn't seat properly from a tight lash adjustment will ultimately burn and fail. Valves need contact with the seat, not only for the obvious compression but also for heat transfer to the seat and water jacket. According to Lunati Cams, valve lash for the 289/302/351W with a flat-tappet mechanical cam is 0.022/0.026 inch intake/exhaust (hot). If you have aluminum heads, which have a greater rate of expansion than iron, allow for expansion.

Proper pushrod length is a very serious consideration for any engine builder. Take a black felt-tip marker and darken the valve-stem tip. Then, install the rocker arm and pushrod. Hand-crank the engine and watch the valve pass through one full opening and closing. Get down alongside the rocker arm and valve spring and watch how the rocker arm travels. Then, inspect the black marking for a wear pattern. This shows you exactly where the rocker-arm tip has traveled across the valve-stem tip. The pattern should be centered on the valve-stem tip. If it runs too much toward the outside of the valve-stem tip, the pushrod is too short. If it runs toward the inside of the valve-stem tip, the pushrod is too long.

INDUCTION

Aside from camshafts, cylinder heads, and the compression ratio, few things affect performance more than induction. I will begin with carburetion, and there are plenty from which to choose. Two basic blueprints are available for performance carburetors: the Holley and Carter aluminum 4-barrel (AFB)/air valve secondary (AVS)–based carburetors.

Ford's Autolite 4100 4V carburetor, also introduced in 1957, has long been a fiercely reliable atomizer with the same footprint as the Holley 1850/4150/4160. Its vacuum secondaries are factory calibrated to come on at just the right vacuum for a smooth transition to wide-open throttle. In addition, it possesses swappable jets and a power valve like the Holley. You're going to want the 600-cfm 4100 for your small-block, although the 289/302s were fitted with a 480-cfm carburetor.

The Autolite 4100 carburetor has a power valve and diaphragm-style accelerator pump like the Holley with vacuum secondaries. This is a terrific factory carburetor. This carburetor holds a good tune and is easy to tune. However, it suffers with age and core shift from heat cycling and plugged passages. Choose the 600-cfm 4100, which was original equipment on the larger 390 big-block.

In 1967, the Autolite/Motorcraft 4300 4-barrel carburetor was introduced as a 441-cfm atomizer for the small-block and big-block as an emissions carburetor. Ford increased it to 600 cfm in 1968. The 4300 has always been a problematic carburetor. It is difficult to tune and was never a performance carburetor to begin with. It is similar to the Rochester Quadrajet in function. The 4300D (for 1971–1972 Boss 351 and High Output engines) has small primaries and large secondaries.

Beginning in 1967, Ford went to the all-new 4300 4-barrel emissions carburetor, which is similar to GM's Rochester Quadrajet. Engineers believed at the time that this was the best approach for the economy, emissions, and performance. Like the Quadrajet, the 4300 had its shortcomings. Technicians and shade-tree mechanics wrestled with the 4300's design shortcomings. The 4300/4300D/4350 have always struggled with drivability issues, including surging, hesitation, and flat spots. At first, the only size that was available was an engine-choking 441-cfm model. In 1968, there was the 600-cfm version.

Carburetor Selection

Holley, of course, remains the hot rodder's choice when it comes to carburetors. They are easy to service at the racetrack, versatile, and handsome for just about any application. You can swap jets, boosters, floats, accelerator pumps, power valves, and more at the racetrack and in the driveway.

Because Holley remains a popular carburetor, performance buffs search high and low for vintage Holleys. I personally admit to being partial to the older Holley castings from the 1960s and 1970s because they are more predictable. However, these old castings can be a crapshoot because they suffer from core shift due to heat cycling and vibration. They also become clogged with debris. See what you can find at swap meets and online auctions.

The popular Holley 1850/4150/4160 has been atomizing fuel and air since 1957, when Ford used this carburetor for its high-performance 312-ci Y-Block V-8 to replace the problematic Teapot "Fire Box" carburetor. The reinvented Holley 1850 was a simple, easy-to-tune 4-barrel carburetor for a broad spectrum of applications.

Many enthusiasts prefer the Carter AFB/AVS–based shoebox carburetors. Edelbrock has taken the time-proven Carter AFB/AVS and refined it. The beauty of the AFB/AVS is also serviceability. You can remove the air horn and not spill one drop of fuel. Jet and metering rod swaps are easy. Most AFB/AVS issues can be solved on the engine.

It is easy to believe that a larger carburetor, more aggressive camshaft, and large-port heads will make more power, but that isn't always true. You can have too much carburetor, which can hinder performance. Larger throttle bores don't always result in more power. They can fall flat on the street because you lose velocity and the corresponding torque at low- to mid-range RPM.

Compromise is essential because radical engines don't do well for the commute or weekend getaway. High-performance engines also struggle to pass a smog check, depending on where you live. Radical camshaft profiles give the engine a rough idle, which can be frustrating in traffic and make it virtually impossible to pass emissions tests. A high compression ratio can cause overheating when traffic comes to a stop. It can also cause destructive spark knock and detonation. Too much carburetion fouls spark plugs and pollutes the air.

Holley

Many owners will probably use an aftermarket intake manifold designed for the Holley 1850/4150/4160 square-flange carburetors or similar aftermarket replacements, such as the AFB and AVS. If you use Holley carburetion, you must understand the differences. The 4150-style carburetor has adjustable metering blocks for the primary and secondary circuits.

The 4160-style carburetor has an adjustable primary metering block and a nonadjustable secondary metering plate. There are single pumpers (a primary accelerator pump) and double pumpers (fully adjustable primary and secondary accelerator pumps).

There are vacuum secondaries and mechanical secondaries. Vacuum secondaries are found mostly on street-performance Holleys, while mechanical secondaries are more

This is the Holley 1850 carburetor, which is the standard replacement for the 4100 and 4300 carburetors. It drops right in place of the factory 4-barrel carburetors.

Enthusiasts like the Holley HP-series carburetors, which have been the performance standard in racing carburetors for nearly two decades. HP carburetors are available from 390 to 1,000 cfm and offer a contoured venturi inlet void of a choke for balanced airflow, screw-in air bleeds for precision tuning capabilities, high-flow metering blocks, and Dominator-style fuel bowls that allow plumbing from either side.

The Holley 4150s and 4160s have side-pivot and cathedral-pivot fuel bowls with this float-needle adjustment, which makes the float adjustment easy. If you install a sight glass in each bowl, you can see the float level without making a mess.

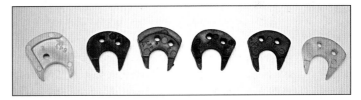

Holley accelerator-pump cams are identified by color and number. Check with holley.com for specifics regarding which cam is required for your application. A total of eight cam options are available in a kit from Holley.

Two Holley accelerator-pump housings and cams are shown side by side. The 50-cc housing (left) calls for the higher-capacity diaphragm.

Holley makes it easy to service carburetors, whether you're going racing or to the office. I like that you can build a complete Holley carburetor from scratch because you can get anything and everything for a build, including the housing, base plate, bowls, metering blocks, floats, jets, boosters, etc.

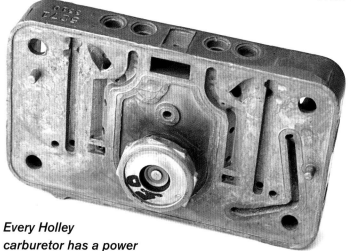

Every Holley carburetor has a power valve, which is located in the metering block. All Holleys have a primary metering block. A secondary metering block is optional and can be added. The power valve's purpose is to improve part-throttle drivability, the air-fuel ratio, and fuel mileage.

Holley has made its share of specialized carburetors (such as the Le Mans–bowl, center-pivot, race-bowl carburetor) for Shelby American and others. The Le Mans bowls aren't cheap. However, they are very effective when road racing. The float control and adjustment don't lose their place with the Le Mans bowl.

race-oriented. Vacuum secondaries come into play as you lean on the throttle under hard acceleration. Mechanical secondaries open immediately with a wide-open throttle.

You will likely never see mechanical secondaries without a secondary accelerator pump. Vacuum-secondary operation depends on the spring pressure and intake manifold vacuum at wide-open throttle. If there is too much spring pressure, the secondaries will barely open or not open at all. If there is too little spring pressure, the secondaries will open too quickly, causing a significant flat spot.

The 4150/4160 carburetors have undergone many changes since the 1950s and 1960s. Each has been offered as original equipment on a variety of factory high-performance engines, including Ford. When you're searching for a good, used, period-correct Holley 4150/4160, it pays to know what you have in your hands. Swap meets are loaded with all types of 4150/4160 carburetors from Holley's good old days.

Edelbrock

Edelbrock carburetors are based on the time-proven, easy-to-tune

Performance Carb in Ontario, California, makes the Holley carburetor even better with specialized performance builds, such as this 750-cfm 4150.

The Holley 4180C is an original-equipment, factory-designed carburetor that was fitted to the 5.0L High Output V-8 from 1983–1985. It is an emissions carburetor that you can tune yourself. This carburetor can be modified with Holley performance parts, such as metering blocks, etc., to get the Holley tune. Note the evaporative emissions vent tubes on the fuel bowls. If you're working with a 1983–1985 Fox Body Mustang, stick with the factory emissions system because it does not adversely affect power.

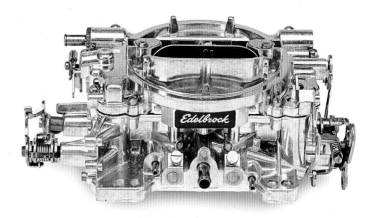

The Edelbrock AVS2-series EnduraShine carburetor is the next generation in Edelbrock carburetors. The AVS2 was designed and calibrated for optimal street performance primarily with small-block V-8 engines. The annular flow-booster design delivers improved fuel atomization to eliminate flat spots.

Edelbrock's Performer-series carburetor is a reliable performance carburetor with a time-proven design. Metering rods are used for a smooth transition between circuits. Because there is no power valve, the Edelbrock Performer isn't affected by sudden engine intake backfire, although modern Holleys have eliminated that concern. In addition, it is compatible with blended methanol fuels.

Carter AFB and AVS. These carburetors perform very well in street/strip applications along with Edelbrock's own performance intake manifolds. Because Edelbrock carburetors function with metering rods and jets instead of power valves, they're unaffected by engine backfire. Edelbrock carburetors are factory-tuned to start right up out of the box, depending upon your elevation and atmospheric conditions.

The Edelbrock Performer and AVS2 carburetors are easy to tune. Metering rods (not shown here) fit into the jet at the bottom of each bowl (white arrows). As the throttle is moved, the metering rods calibrate the flow of fuel. Metering rods are tapered to adjust the fuel flow, depending upon demand. Idle-air-mixture screws (black arrows) control the idle mixture.

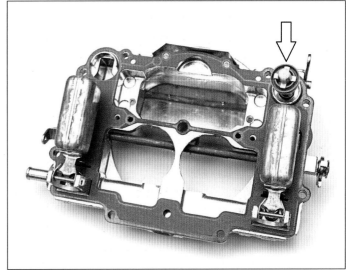

The Edelbrock's air horn consists of two brass floats and the accelerator-pump piston (arrow). Remove the air horn to make changes and adjustments without spilling fuel.

There are two types of Edelbrock carburetors: the Performer series and the Thunder AVS series. Sizing ranges from 500 to 850 cfm. The 1400 Performer-series carburetor with electric choke delivers reliable street performance in daily driving. The biggest plus of the Performer is that metering rods transition between the idle and power circuits. These metering rods can be changed in seconds without carburetor removal or fuel draining.

The Thunder AVS allows for a smooth transition from primary to wide-open throttle (just like the Performer) due to the Qwik-Tune vacuum-secondary air valve, which delivers a more precise throttle response. The Edelbrock Thunder-series AVS electric-choke carburetor has been designed and calibrated to deliver real off-road performance. What this means to you is that performance remains consistent and the calibration stays unchanged in street and off-road driving.

Carter

The Carter AFB and AVS 4-barrel carburetors have also been around since 1957. The AFB and AVS were not only original equipment in a lot of automobiles but they also became something of a performance standard for racers and street enthusiasts alike. Carter has been gone since 1985. However, there are untold millions of Carter AFB and AVS carburetors.

Chrysler and GM employed the AFB/AVS on many vintage muscle cars, but Ford never did (with Lincoln being the only exception). That doesn't mean that you can't run it on your small-block Ford. The appeal of the AFB and AVS is how easy they are to service and tune. As with the popular Edelbrock Performer and Thunder AVS-series carburetors, the Carter AFB/AVS carburetors work on metering rods and jets for ease of tuning. There's no concern about fuel spillage when service is performed because these carburetors are like a bathtub. You can swap jets and metering rods without spilling a drop. There's also no power valve to sweat out either, although Holley's power valves are now designed to be resistant to backfires.

Federal Mogul acquired Carter in 1986 and continued to manufacture the AFB and AVS along with other popular Carter models. That continued until 2013 when Carter was sold to a private-equity firm. In 2018, Carter was acquired by Trico.

Demon

Demon, a division of Holley, remains uniquely Demon with a wide variety of performance carburetors for a broad spectrum of budgets. Street Demons and Road Demons are both Holley- and Carter-based atomizers in terms of design but are actually quite different in terms of performance and function.

Architecturally, the Street Demon is Carter-based and available in 625- and 750-cfm sizes. The Road Demon is Holley-based and available in 650-, 750-, and 850-cfm sizes. The Street Demon and Road Demon are available in black and aluminum finishes. All have suitable Ford throttle and kickdown linkages and are among the easiest carburetors to tune.

The Screamin' Demon, Mighty Demon, and Race Demon kick it up a few notches in terms of performance. Holley is proud to announce the next generation of Mighty Demon carburetors. These race-oriented Demon carburetors are available in a wide range of sizes and options for your street/strip car. You get a billet-aluminum metering block, billet-aluminum baseplates, large-capacity fuel bowls (complete with dual sight glasses), dual threaded inlets on each side, and internal baffling to prevent fuel slosh when you are on the track.

Quick Fuel Technology

Quick Fuel Technology, also a division of Holley, needs little introduction with performance enthusiasts. These are simply great carburetors. You never have to wonder if they're okay out of the box. Quick Fuel Technology's Slayer-series street carburetors are designed with many of the same innovations and features that are built into all its race-winning carburetors, including changeable air bleeds and power-valve channel restrictions. The Slayer is fully tunable with a secondary metering block with swappable jets and all-aluminum construction for additional weight savings.

The Hot Rod (HR)–series carburetor is a truly versatile performer for a broad spectrum of engines. It features lightweight die-cast aluminum components and tunability that you would expect from more expensive racing carburetors, including changeable bleeds, idle feed, power-valve channel restrictions, and four-corner idle adjustment. Offered with either vacuum or mechanical secondary models, all HR-series carburetors feature electric chokes and dual metering blocks for tunability.

Weber

The Weber IDA, IDF, and DCOE carburetors are good-looking, twin-bore carburetors that have experienced great success around the world. However, they are not for everyone.

Using Weber carburetion has always been a popular small-block modification, although it is expensive and time-consuming to tune. Weber carburetors also call for a Weber-specific intake manifold.

This is the very limited production Autolite Inline 4-barrel carburetor that was produced for road racing from 1969 to 1970. This exotic piece calls for its own intake manifold for very limited applications, such as the Boss 302 and 429. Although a fortunate few run it on the street and on the track, it is not a practical fuel system for street and weekend racers.

You must know what you're doing, otherwise count on a frustrating experience trying to tune them.

The beauty of Weber carburetors is how well they mix fuel and air before it all reaches the venturi. Another positive is how tunable the Weber is with a wide variety of jets and venturis available to get it right where you want it. Although the Weber really is a racing carburetor, it can be operated on the street.

Weber caught the close attention of Carroll Shelby, who decided to place a quartet of these carburetors on top of Ford's 260-ci V-8 in the early 1960s, giving Ford's small-block a 30-hp advantage. The nice thing about the Weber is the fuel/air distribution because each bore has its own bore, or eight throttle bores for eight cylinders, offering perfect fuel distribution.

Weber carburetors do not have a choke. Instead, they have a fuel-enrichment system that functions when the engine is cold. As with most carburetors, Webers have an accelerator pump, which sprays raw fuel into the throttle bore when the throttle is advanced. The trick with Webers is getting them in sync with each other.

Carburetor Size

Carburetor sizing is something that few people get right. It is not for the novice. However, it is very important to performance and durability. Before you can determine what size carburetor you need, you must know the maximum airflow your engine requires. This may seem like a simple task, but it isn't. When you do the simple math of computing carburetor size, you've only scratched the surface. Then, you need to know how the engine will be used, the engine's operational window, and the number of cylinders. This is where it gets even trickier.

Flow Rating (CFM) at 3.0 in/Hg ÷ 1.414 = Flow (CFM) at 1.5 in/Hg
Flow Rating (CFM) at 1.5 in/Hg ÷ 1.414 = Flow (CFM) at 3.0 in/Hg

These formulas are based on the presumed maximum vacuum that is attainable under load at wide-open throttle. In theory, an engine won't realize manifold vacuum of more than 1.5 in/Hg with a 4-barrel carburetor or more than 3.0 in/Hg with a 2-barrel carburetor. Carburetor manufacturers and car magazines can suggest carburetor sizing based on loose information. However, each engine is different, even if they are identically equipped.

Carburetor airflow ratings don't always match how much a given carburetor will flow. With that being said, carburetor sizing guidelines aren't always absolute. Instead, they're suggestions to get you close. According to Dave Emanuel, who wrote *How to Rebuild and Modify Carter/Edelbrock Carburetors* for CarTech, sizing depends on displacement and volumetric efficiency (VE).

It also depends on the vehicle type, weight, size, transmission gearing, and the axle ratio. However, let's keep it simple. You want to know what your small-block's maximum RPM range will be coupled with where it's going to be, (RPM-wise) most of the time.

Use this basic formula and see how it fits your plan.

$$351 \text{ ci} \times 6{,}000 \text{ rpm} \div 3{,}456 = 609.375 \text{ cfm}$$

This means that the average high-performance street small-block needs 600 to 650 cfm. It is when you get into high RPM and greater displacement that more CFM (a larger carburetor) is needed. Let's say that you're working with a 351W and the engine is going to make most of its power in the form of torque between 2,000 and 5,000 rpm. You're not going to need much more than 650 cfm. If you're going to take the engine above 6,000 rpm, you're talking 750 cfm.

When you get on the dyno, you start thinking of air/fuel ratio and VE. VE is the percentage of the theoretical maximum amount of air and fuel that can be drawn into an engine during two complete crankshaft revolutions. What does this really mean? It means that if you take a 351-ci engine and turn the crank two revolutions, you should get 351 ci of air. This doesn't happen in the real world. In fact, VE varies a lot throughout RPM ranges under load in dyno testing.

It is true that most engines experience a VE number of 70 to 80 percent at maximum engine speed. Racing engines at high revs average 85- to 90-percent VE. If you're really on top of your game as an engine builder and tuner, you can achieve 90- to 110-percent VE at high RPM with a racing engine.

To figure potential VE numbers, here's the equation:

$$351 \text{ ci} \times 6{,}500 \text{ rpm} = 2{,}281{,}500 \div 3{,}456 = 660.156 \times 1.1 \text{ VE} = 726.172$$

In theory, a 750-cfm carburetor would be the right size. However, other variables in the real world either raise or lower this number, including the header-tube size and length, collector size, exhaust-pipe size, intake-manifold type, cylinder heads, ambient temperature and humidity, engine temperature, and more. Keep proper carburetor jetting in mind too. Always err on the side of rich versus lean for longer engine life. A true measure of the mixture is more wide-open throttle versus light throttle. Light-to-normal throttle doesn't provide an accurate measure of the mixture.

Remember, if you're building a stroker, think larger engine. You don't have a 351 anymore—you have a 408 or a 427. Even though it remains a small-block, it has greater displacement.

Carburetor Spacers

Carburetor spacers are always a topic of conversation for enthusiasts. Their worth has been proven in dyno testing. Carburetor-spacer design and width is where it gets involved. How wide should you go? Do you want open plenum or four-hole? Do you want custom-shaped bores? There's a lot to think about. How well carburetor spacers perform is a matter of opinion and what you get

Carburetor spacers insulate engine heat from the carburetor. However, they also improve velocity as atomized fuel and air leaves the carburetor and enters the intake plenum. I've never seen a situation where a carburetor spacer reduced power. If you have the luxury of a large budget, you can test various spacer thicknesses and record the results.

from the dyno sheets. Factor in humidity levels, barometric pressure, and temperature, and it can vary widely.

The late Marlan Davis, technical editor at *Hot Rod* magazine, said that carburetor spacers were believed to improve air/fuel vaporization within and outside of the carburetor. He said that any time the air/fuel charge turns sharply coming off the carburetor, it increases the chance of separating the fuel and air, which hurts power.

By raising the carburetor higher off the manifold, there's more time for the fuel to gently turn into the intake runners and less chance of the charge to bounce sharply off the plenum floor. Additionally, changing the effective intake-plenum volume and height with a spacer may change the intake manifold's tuning resonance, which is somewhat analogous to playing with exhaust header-tube and collector lengths and volumes. Spacers also have an insulating affect. They tend to cool the air/fuel charge.

Davis said that a given spacer may help at the top of the curve but at the expense of the bottom of the curve. That could be good or bad, depending on the end goal of power.

"Garnering a little more top end at the expense of the bottom end generally has little downside at the drags [assuming no throttle-stop] or in land-speed racing," Davis said. "However, that's not the case for other venues or on the street.

"A spacer may not show anything on the dyno at full throttle, but in the real world it still could improve part-throttle response and/or the transition from part to full throttle. This can be important on a dual-purpose street car or in closed-course racing (ovals, road courses, slaloms, or rallying)."

Unfortunately, most dynos are capable of only full-throttle testing, Davis said.

Hood-clearance permitting, a taller spacer is typically better than a short spacer. The farther away the carburetor boosters are from the intake valve, the more the air/fuel droplets have time to vaporize as they make their way through the plenum and runners. This gives them more time to lose heat and be chilled. Two-inch-tall spacers are generally a good baseline-height choice for race cars. Street/strip cars typically have hood clearance issues.

Four-hole spacers help low-end torque with velocity (air speed) by correcting the air/fuel slipstream coming out of the carburetor. They also tend to enhance fuel vaporization time by moving the boosters farther away from the manifold runners. Open spacers (plenums) add more top-end power. However, they typically trade off lower-RPM performance. Wilson Manifolds' unique carburetor spacers are either a two- or four-hole configuration on top, tapering into a semi-open-but-tapered configuration down below, above the intake plenum. Wilson Manifolds states that it combines the best attributes of open and closed spacers to enhance part-throttle and full-throttle performance.

Keep in mind that the use of a spacer may alter throttle-linkage geometries. Some fabrication may be necessary.

Intake Manifold

A simple formula for selecting an intake manifold is knowing what type of driving you're going to do. Street and weekend racing calls for a good dual-plane intake manifold, such as the Edelbrock Performer series or the classic F4B manifold. These manifolds, with their long runners, provide good low- to mid-range torque and a nice broad torque curve that comes on strong from 2,500–3,500 rpm.

Single-plane intake manifolds, such as the Edelbrock Victor series or the classic Torkers and Streetmasters, are strictly high-RPM manifolds with open plenums and short runners. Short runners and a straight-in shot work best at high RPM. However, the classic Streetmaster provides both mid-range and high-end power because it has long runners, yet it is a single-plane manifold.

Long intake runners and a dual-plane design are only two reasons why good low- and mid-range torque can be achieved from a carbureted engine. Edelbrock's Air Gap family of dual-plane intake manifolds cool the plenum and the runners to provide power from the cooler air/fuel charge. Thermal expansion brings more out of the air/fuel combination as it enters the chambers.

You also want cool air both ahead of the carburetor and beneath it. To get cool air before the carburetor, you need to source cool air from outside. Under-hood air is much hotter than the ambient air outside. On a hot day, it becomes even more challenging. If you can drop the intake air temperature by 50°F to

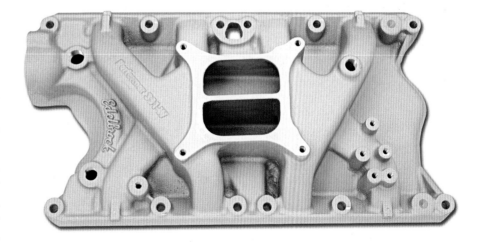

The very basic Edelbrock Performer 351W is a drop-in replacement for the cast-iron 4V intake. It doesn't offer the benefits of the Performer RPM manifolds, but it runs cooler and offers improved flow. (Photo Courtesy Edelbrock)

With the Performer RPM, Edelbrock raised the runner ceilings, which is good for high-RPM power. In addition, this manifold still gives you good low-end torque for the street. (Photo Courtesy Edelbrock)

If you opt for Cleveland heads on a small-block, use the appropriate intake manifold. The Edelbrock E-Boss 302 enables you to run the 351C head with its generous ports and poly-angle valves. (Photo Courtesy Edelbrock)

Edelbrock's Performer RPM Air Gap for the 289/302 is a nice upgrade because you get airflow and a cooler intake charge, which provides more power. The cooler the charge, the greater the thermal expansion when it hits the chambers. These manifolds are a bit taller than the regular RPM manifolds, so care must be taken regarding hood clearance. (Photo Courtesy Edelbrock)

When high-RPM racing performance is the goal, the Victor Jr.–series single-plane manifolds work well. A single-plane manifold offers a straight shot from the plenum into the ports. The single-plane design and short runners are optimal for high-RPM power. (Photo Courtesy Edelbrock)

All-out racing calls for the Super Victor 8.2, which is a tall single-plane manifold that lives happily at 8,000 to 9,000 rpm. (Photo Courtesy Edelbrock)

80°F, this will make a considerable difference in thermal expansion inside of the combustion chamber. Cooler air comes from a hood scoop or a ram-air scoop at the leading edge of the vehicle. Ram air can be sourced through the radiator support or beneath the front bumper. Ram-air kits can be sourced from your favorite speed shop.

The small-block Ford's factory induction system changed dramatically when Ford went to sequential electronic fuel injection (SEFI) in 1986. When Ford introduced SEFI, its new induction system got a laugh from enthusiasts because it looked more like a vacuum-cleaner rug attachment than a manifold. This design was due to distributor-clearance issues and the need for long intake runners for good low- to mid-range torque. The aftermarket offers a wealth of terrific high-performance induction systems for the 5.0L and 5.8L engines.

The Edelbrock Performer RPM II is vastly improved over the existing Edelbrock 5.0L High Output designs in the 1,500 to 6,500 rpm range, which makes it ideal for street and strip. Edelbrock offers a 70-mm throttle body for this application (75 mm requires port matching).

The Edelbrock Pro-Flo 4 XT EFI system has the traditional 4150/4160 square-flange, single-plane intake manifold with eight 29-lb/hr injectors and is capable of 450 hp. You also get a plug-and-play, single-connection distributor that is designed to work specifically with the Pro-Flo system. This is a good way to get into EFI.

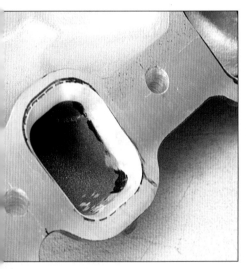

Perform a good port match between the heads and intake using manifold gaskets as a template. Scribe lines in both the intake and heads for a perfect match.

Bolt-on EFI

If you are weary of carburetion and the tuning and retuning that goes with it, the aftermarket yields plenty of bolt-on electronic-fuel-injection (EFI) options. Your choices are throttle-body injection (TBI) or port fuel injection. Both are quite simple to install and tune. In addition, they self-tune upon answering a body of questions to where the system self learns and runs like clockwork once it understands what's expected. Once the system is familiar with your engine and driving habits, simply turn the key, and it fires.

Selecting an aftermarket EFI system boils down to your knowledge of these systems and how proficient you are with automotive electrical and fuel systems. It is good to have some fabrication skills too. You need a support system (an in-tank or inline pump) along with an independent electrical circuit that is fuse or circuit-breaker protected. You need a fuel filter that is designed for high-pressure fuel injection. Count on needing an impact switch, which kills the pump in a crash.

Summit's MAX-efi 500 TBI system is the most affordable at less than $1,000. The Summit system is the most efficient way to convert a carbureted small-block Ford to EFI with a minimum of fuss and expense. The self-tuning throttle body bolts directly to Holley 4150/4160 square-flange manifolds. Then, via the oxygen sensor and microprocessor, it continually adjusts fuel delivery to provide the optimal air/fuel ratio under all climate and altitude conditions. It can support 500 hp and offers a limp-home mode if you get into trouble.

Holley's Sniper EFI TBI system is a simple bolt-on system that involves few modifications, including an in-tank or inline pump, oxygen-sensor installation into one of the two exhaust pipes just aft of the header or manifold, and doing a nice, neat job of routing the harnesses. The same can be said for Fi-Tech's TBI system, which is easy to install and tune once the infrastructure is in place. There's also MSD's Atomic EFI TBI system, which offers many of the same functions and features as the competition.

Edelbrock, which pioneered bolt-on aftermarket EFI, offers the Pro-Flo 4 EFI system, which provides easy installation via a throttle body and eight port injectors for straight-shot operation. Unlike most throttle-body EFI systems, Pro-Flo 4

I have personally worked with the Holley Sniper EFI system on early small-block Fords, and the results have been remarkable. FiTech is another option for those who are looking for reliable and efficient EFI. No more carburetor issues—just turn the key and go. You have a number of fuel tank and pump options.

has fuel rails and individual injectors for each port mounted on the manifold. What this means for you is good fuel atomization and distribution.

Before you invest in an EFI system, shop the internet, look at the reviews, and make an educated decision on what will work best for your small-block in terms of performance and reliability.

EFI Throttle-Body Sizing

Before packaging an EFI induction system, determine what your engine is going to need for a throttle body. The size depends on the displacement, cylinder heads, cam profile, and RPM that are expected. If you've taken your 302 to 347 ci or a 351W to 427 ci, you now have a larger displacement and must handle your build accordingly. The cam profile (aggressiveness) and RPM that is expected also affects throttle-body sizing.

Author and technical writer Richard Holdener, who wrote *How to Build New Hemi Performance on the Dyno, Building 4.6/5.4L Ford Horsepower on the Dyno*, and more for CarTech, possesses a massive amount of dyno-room experience. He wrote in *Hot Rod* magazine that a throttle-body swap he performed netted over 60 hp on a Kenne Bell supercharged application. However, the question was not so much, "Can a throttle-body swap net a sizable jump in power?" but rather, "Does such a throttle-body upsize always result in big gains?"

"In its simplest form, the throttle body is nothing more than an air valve," Holdener said. "There is no magic to the workings of a throttle body, although there is some magic to maximizing the flow rate through it. A given opening will flow a certain amount of air, but radiused entries, thin throttle blades, and the elimination of hardware in the air stream all combine to further increase the airflow of a given bore size. It stands to reason that a 90-mm throttle

body should outflow an 80-mm throttle body, but it is possible for a well-designed 80-mm throttle body to outflow a poorly-designed 90-mm throttle body."

According to Holdener, once you have established that a larger throttle body will outflow a smaller version (assuming equal design quality), you can then look at why the installation of a larger throttle body may or may not improve power. It tends to be trial and error in addition to using the math. There are several approaches to TBI. It is true that using dual throttle bodies is the most common approach with factory production engines. The throttle body to the port looks exotic and seems to work best. One single throttle body is the simplest solution, which is tied directly to a common intake manifold.

The overall length of the induction system runners is critical to power. Runners that are too short will lose power. Short runners are good for high-RPM power—as long

This is a 75-mm BBK throttle body for the 5.0L High Output engine. Throttle-body sizing comes from the internal bore size in millimeters. A throttle body that is too large reduces low-end torque while coming on strong at high RPM.

as you don't go too short. This is best learned on the dyno and in real-world use. However, few of us have the budget to try different intake manifolds. One reference source stated that 350 mm from the plenum to the valve face is optimal for 9,000-rpm power. Not many small-block Fords are going to reach 9,000 rpm.

Fuel Injectors

Two basic types of fuel injectors are available for the small-block Ford: the Bosch EV1 with a two-pin connector (OEM on 1986–1993 5.0L High Output engines) and the Bosch EV6. The EV1s were produced in different flow ratings and are identifiable by color. The Bosch EV6, which arrived in 1992, is a better, pencil-thin injector with a United States Council for Automotive Research (USCAR) two-pin plug. If you want to switch over to an EV6 injector, use the Ford Performance M-14464-A8 adaptor kit.

Regardless of what type of fuel injector you use, here's what you need for a given amount of power. Fuel injectors are sized by how much fuel they flow. The flow rate is a measurement of how much fuel can be delivered over time in pounds per hour (lbs/hr) or cubic centimeters per minute (cc/min). A correctly sized injector can supply enough fuel under full-load conditions at an 80-percent duty cycle. This allows the injector to close 20 percent of the time at wide-open throttle, which prevents overheating. An injector of this size can also provide an accurate amount of fuel at low RPM.

For example, using 500 hp (naturally aspirated) as the objective, the first thing to address is brake specific fuel consumption (BSFC). BSFC refers to the amount of fuel that an engine

The injector sizing and type depends on the amount of power that you intend to make. For example, let's use a 5.0L High Output engine with 220 hp. Take (215 x 0.55) ÷ (8 x 0.80) = 18.5 lb/hr. You need 19-lb/hr injectors. David Fuller of OnAllCylinders said that if you have a 275-hp Ford small-block, you take (275 x 0.50) ÷ (8 x 0.85) = 20.1 lbs/hr. You likely want 24-lbs/hr injectors.

will produce as 1 hp in 1 hour and is expressed in pounds of fuel per horsepower per hour.

To ascertain proper injector sizing, use this formula.

$$(Horsepower \times BSFC) \div (Number\ of\ Injectors \times Injector\ Duty\ Cycle)$$

For example, a naturally aspirated, 300-hp engine (BSFC 0.5) with eight fuel injectors needs 23.4 lbs/hr of fuel per injector at an 80-percent (0.8) duty cycle.

$$(300 \times 0.5) \div (8 \times 0.8) = 23.4\ lbs/hr$$

This formula gets you into the ballpark size wise. Then, you can calibrate fuel pressure to get it where you need it or consider swapping fuel-injector size up or down. A pro-

fessional tuner can then get it where it needs to be.

Sizing Fuel Injectors		
Injector Flow Rate (Pounds/Hr)	Naturally Aspirated (Horsepower)	Boost or Power Adders (Horsepower)
19	225–290	185–240
24	280–360	240–300
30	350–450	300–375
36	425–540	350–450
42	500–625	410–525
46	540–690	450–575
52	610–775	510–650
60	710–900	590–750

(Table Courtesy Summit Racing Equipment)

If you select an injector that's not large enough, you won't have the power at wide-open throttle. Worse yet, you will be too lean, which can cause severe engine damage. Finally, injector longevity goes right out the window. If you opt for an injector that's too large, low-end power will suffer. Engine life will be shortened by oil being washed off the cylinder walls. Expect excessive spark-plug fouling.

Because fuel injectors are quite expensive, you want to get this right the first time. This is one reason why you want to consult with a seasoned and reputable professional tuner before making the investment.

Supercharging and Turbocharging

As with nitrous-oxide injection, supercharging and turbocharging were conceived a long time ago to extract as much power as possible from a given displacement. Unlike nitrous, supercharging and turbocharging require a more involved installation, but they are easier to tune and manage.

Supercharging and turbocharging both force air into the cylinders to make the most of the combustion power cycle. They mechanically increase cylinder pressure, which, given enough fuel, makes more power. Superchargers are driven by the engine's crankshaft. Turbochargers are driven by exhaust gas.

Turbochargers take a certain amount of time to provide induction pressure when you step on the gas. This is called "turbo lag." Because it takes the turbocharger time to spool up during acceleration, there is a certain amount of lag before getting the boost pressure and the resulting power. Turbochargers have a wastegate, which also bleeds excessive boost pressure to prevent engine damage.

A wide variety of supercharging systems is available for the small-block Ford. If you have room, intercooled supercharger systems yield the most power and boost for the money. For example, Vortech has offered a wide variety of supercharger systems for more than 25 years. Order a system that is smog legal for your state. The nice thing about Vortech is that it is a system you can build on and add to.

There are six basic different types of superchargers: centrifugal, rotary, axial flow, Roots two-lobe, Roots three-lobe, the vane type, and the Lysholm screw. Probably the most common types on small-block Fords are centrifugal and Roots. Centrifugal superchargers are typically installed on the front of the engine and are belt driven by the crankshaft pulley. Roots blowers, which are also driven by the crankshaft pulley, are normally an integral part of the intake manifold, with the carburetor mounted immediately upwind of the blower. With fuel injection, the throttle body is mounted in any number of locations before the Roots blower's intake. Fuel injectors are positioned in each of the intake ports downwind of the Roots blower.

A Roots blower is effective due to its positive-displacement design, which a Detroit two-stroke diesel engine needs for proper ingestion of air and scavenging of exhaust gasses. This kind of positive-displacement design ascertains plenty of cylinder pressure when and where it counts in a high-performance engine.

Turbochargers are similar to centrifugal superchargers because they work much the same way. Instead of being belt-driven, they're driven by a turbine that is propelled by hot exhaust gasses. During acceleration, hot exhaust gasses drive the turbocharger's single-stage turbine, which drives the centrifugal compressor.

In author Bob McClurg's *How to Build Supercharged & Turbocharged Small-Block Fords* book from CarTech, he explains boost.

"There's a significant difference

in the calculated static compression ratio and the dynamic compression ratio. When you pencil out a static compression ratio, you compare the volume of air that the piston's movement will displace with the volume of air that will exist between the piston dome and the combustion chamber surfaces at TDC. In supercharged applications, however, the chamber volume will be included in the displaced volume, increasing the BDC displacement figure without an associated increase in the TDC volume. This effectively increases the compression ratio, at least under boost.

"To optimize a supercharged engine, reducing the static compression ratio will allow higher intake-manifold pressure (more boost) without wandering into problems with detonation. Unfortunately, having too low of a static ratio can affect drivability. If the vehicle will be expected to negotiate traffic most of the time, the static compression ratio must suit those conditions and be high enough to maintain adequate spark-plug and combustion-chamber temperatures for low-speed operation. This usually requires a compression ratio above 8.0:1.

"To allow higher boost levels, the static compression ratio can be set at approximately 7.5:1 with pistons having shorter compression heights than stock. This ratio is useable on the street only if the engine is exercised on a regular basis. Otherwise, you'll be changing fouled spark plugs a lot more often than you'll care to.

"The fuel requirement of a supercharged engine is not precisely related to the increased volume of air under boost. Programming the fuel curve to reflect the increased airflow using the fuel requirements of a non-supercharged engine will result in a very lean mixture under heavy boost. The additional fuel required under heavy boost often calls for an auxiliary fuel pump to control the combustion temperature in the chambers.

"While the excess fuel in the engine will absorb large amounts of heat in the process of achieving optimal fuel vaporization, if oxygen no longer remains in the chamber to support combustion, the vaporized (and usually some raw) fuel will leave through the exhaust valve. But without what sounds like a wasteful process, the engine would self-destruct under detonation."

Nitrous Oxide

Nitrous oxide, or "squeeze," is popular today for those looking for quick and easy power (50 to 150 hp) on demand. However, nitrous oxide can be very harmful to an engine that isn't properly prepared and tuned. Nitrous oxide can severely damage pistons, rings, and bearings if not properly used. It can (and does) hammer rod and main bearings. No matter what the nitrous-oxide crowd says, nitrous oxide can shorten engine life.

What is nitrous oxide and how does it make power? Nitrous oxide requires a physics lesson on how to generate greater amounts of power from the fuel/air charge that is introduced to the engine. Nitrous oxide is a very simple gas that is composed of two nitrogen atoms attached to one oxygen atom. Chemists call it N_2O. Contrary to what you may believe about N_2O, it is not a poisonous gas, nor is it harmful to the atmosphere. Because N_2O is an asphyxiant, it can suffocate you if it is inhaled in heavy quantities (oxygen deprivation). It has a similar effect as carbon dioxide (CO_2).

Nitrous oxide is available in three basic grades: medical, commercial, and high purity. The medical grade is commonly known as laughing gas and is used by dentists and surgeons. It has to be very pure for human consumption. You must be licensed as a medical professional to get it. Commercial-grade nitrous oxide is used in engines for performance gains. High-purity nitrous oxide is also a medical-grade gas that is extremely pure. It is priced and controlled accordingly.

Commercial-grade nitrous oxide is marketed as "Nytrous+" and is sold by the Puritan-Bennett Corporation. You can find it all across the country. It is a mix of 99.9-percent nitrous oxide and 0.01 percent sulfur dioxide. Puritan-Bennett adds the sulfur dioxide to give the N_2O gas an odor, just like natural gas.

The use of nitrous oxide to make power is nothing new. In World War II, it was used to help aircraft engines make power. The principle then was much the same as it is now. Nitrous oxide was stored under pressure in tanks, much as it is today. Nitrous oxide stored under pressure must be anchored securely. I stress safety because a carelessly handled nitrous-oxide bottle with nearly 1,000 psi of pressure behaves like a bomb if the bottle fails.

To get the nitrous oxide that is necessary for performance use on demand, the gas is metered from the bottle via electrical solenoids that are fired when the button is depressed. Nitrous oxide should be administered on demand at a time when it is safe to do so. Too much nitrous oxide and not enough fuel can destroy an engine. Nitrous oxide

Nitrous oxide appears to be a fast answer for quick power. However, with nitrous oxide comes responsibility. Horsepower and torque are not free. If you use nitrous oxide, the engine and nitrous-oxide system must be in a good state of tune and in a healthy condition. Watch working compression and keep it conservative. Detonation will blow the engine.

should never be administered to the intake ports unless the throttle is wide open. When it has been set up properly, the throttle should close a nitrous-oxide-solenoid switch when it is in the wide-open position.

A popular misconception is that power comes from the nitrous oxide itself. But this isn't true. Nitrous oxide works hand in hand with the fuel/air mix to make power in each cylinder bore. Nitrous oxide brings out the best in the fuel. Not only is the nitrous oxide mist cold (good for thermal expansion), it is also loaded with oxygen, which gives the igniting fuel/air mix a bad attitude. It makes the fuel/air mix burn faster, which creates a powerful

thermal-expansion experience in each combustion chamber.

Safety

The first thing to remember with nitrous oxide is that it makes fuel burn faster. This means that you must be mindful of what it can do—both positively and negatively. Administering nitrous oxide to the combustion chambers should not be done with reckless abandon. When tuning a small-block Ford to run on nitrous oxide, you must get the fuel/air mixture and spark timing where they need to be. Otherwise, you will face severe engine damage. Fuel delivery must be controlled to where it is at the correct ratio with the flow of nitrous oxide. If you get too

much N_2O in there and not enough fuel, you overheat the chamber and damage the pistons. This means that you have to control fuel and nitrous oxide flow to a finite point where you get the most power possible without damaging the engine.

The key to getting the most power from nitrous oxide is getting spark timing, fuel delivery, and peak cylinder pressure going at the same time. Ideally, you light the fuel/air/nitrous oxide mixture at the time when there is peak cylinder pressure, which makes the most of the incoming charge.

Compression is thought of in two ways: static and dynamic compression. Static compression is the compression ratio. This is the swept volume above the piston with the piston at BDC versus the clearance volume left when the piston is at TDC. If you have 100 cc of volume with the piston at BDC and 10 cc left with the piston at TDC, you have a static compression ratio of 10.0:1 (100 cc to 10 cc).

Dynamic compression happens with the engine running. This is the kind of compression that happens with pistons, valves, and gasses in motion. You get dynamic compression when you are moving a lot of air through the engine. With the engine running, you are pumping more volume through the cylinders and chambers than you would cranking the engine. This actually increases compression ratio, which means that dynamic compression is higher than static compression. It means that you need to consider the dynamic compression ratio as your engine's actual compression when you're planning nitrous oxide. The compression ratio must be handled similarly to how it is with the boost of supercharging and turbocharging applications. It should be around 7.5:1 to 8.5:1. This is okay for racing applications, but for street applications, you are giving up power for the times when you are not on the button, which is most of the time.

The dynamic compression ratio is affected by the camshaft profile. A camshaft profile with a short duration results in greater dynamic compression. When the duration is lengthened, you tend to lose dynamic compression. On the exhaust side, duration is very important with nitrous oxide. Because the fuel/air/nitrous oxide charge coming in expands with fury during compression/ignition, it needs a way to escape when the exhaust valve opens. You need longer exhaust-valve duration with nitrous oxide for good scavenging and the thorough extraction of power, which is why nitrous cams are ground differently.

Valve overlap is also important in all of this. With less overlap, there is more dynamic compression. With more overlap, there is less dynamic compression. Overlap is that process in the power cycle where the exhaust valve is closing and the intake valve is opening. The incoming charge helps scavenge the outgoing hot gasses through the overlap process. What this means is simple. It means that the exhaust valve needs to open earlier in the cycle and stay open longer for adequate scavenging.

If your tuning effort involves a carburetor, get jet sizing down to a science to help the engine live on nitrous oxide. As a rule, carbureted engines live happily with an air/fuel ratio of 12.5:1 to 13.0:1. If you go any leaner, nitrous oxide can cause engine damage.

When working with a fuel-injected engine, you can control the fuel mixture by reprogramming the electronic control module (ECM) or changing the injector size. With nitrous oxide, I typically go up on injector size and fine tune from there. Too large is better than too small. Factory fuel-injection systems run a fuel-manifold pressure of 30 to 45 psi. When running nitrous oxide, you need a lot more fuel pressure to get the job done safely. Around 80 psi is considered the norm for nitrous oxide and electronic fuel injection.

Ignition timing is next because it can damage an engine as quickly as a lean fuel mixture or too much compression when running nitrous oxide. The spark should occur in advance of peak cylinder pressure because it takes time for the fuel/air/nitrous-oxide mixture to ignite. Under normal circumstances, without nitrous oxide, you want full spark advance around 36 to 41 degrees BTDC.

With nitrous oxide, the air/fuel/nitrous-oxide mixture that is going to ignite more rapidly than the conventional fuel/air mix. Tuning professionals suggest retarding the ignition timing to approximately 12 degrees BTDC because the air/fuel/nitrous-oxide mixture ignites much more quickly. With full spark advance at 36 to 41 degrees BTDC, the engine would surely fail. Retard timing to 12 degrees BTDC and go from there. Twelve degrees BTDC at 3,500 rpm should be the baseline. Then, slowly advance ignition timing from there. Test it at wide-open throttle under a load beginning at 12 degrees BTDC, and then advance from there 1 degree at a time.

IGNITION

Ignition systems must be pinpoint accurate with potent spark timing to ensure smooth light-off and power. It's easy to light the air/fuel mixture at low RPM, but it gets tricky at high RPM, where conditions change dramatically. When thinking about how engines work, it may seem like just the simple four-cycle process: intake, compression/ignition, combustion/power stroke, and exhaust. However, it gets more complicated. Because the physics are more involved, it is the precise timing of these four events that determines how reliably an engine will perform.

Fuel and air ignite in a quick fire, which is a light-off across the piston dome that begins at the ignition source. The ignition of fuel and air begins at the ignition source, whether it's a spark plug or a red-hot piece of carbon. As the fuel/air mix ignites, it flashes and expands across the chamber at a rate of about 700 feet per second and acts on the piston, rod, and crank.

Because fuel and air ignite in a quick fire, time is required for this thermal reaction to happen. The spark plug doesn't fire when the piston reaches TDC. Instead, it fires a few degrees BTDC because fuel needs time to ignite and react. This ignition process happens in a nanosecond, even at idle. At high RPM, it happens in a fraction of a nanosecond and must happen earlier in the compression/ignition cycle. Under optimal conditions, there is a smooth light-off and a generous outpouring of power.

Where this becomes even more complex is the cam profile, combustion-chamber size and shape, valve size and shape, and the dynamic and static compression ratios. It gets even more confusing when identical engines with the same ignition timing don't offer the same reaction or power. That's because no two engines are the same. There are just enough variables that each engine mandates its own tuning agenda, even if you're working with identical engines.

When adjusting ignition timing, it must be performed with a timing light and an accurate harmonic damper. Are your harmonic damper timing marks properly indexed? Even a new harmonic damper must be examined for proper indexing. I've seen them as much as 11 degrees off.

Even in its day, the single-point Autolite/Motorcraft distributor wasn't impressive. It suffered from poor shaft support (a single bushing), which caused point bounce at high RPM. Ford later compensated with a second shaft bushing, which didn't change the dynamics much.

Ford took the same basic distributor and made it a dual-point unit for high-performance engines. It did a good job in its day. However, the aftermarket has answered the call with better high-performance ignitions.

Beginning in 1968, Ford went to an advance/retard distributor known as IMCO (improved combustion), which advanced or retarded the spark in relation to the throttle position, manifold vacuum, and coolant temperature. A thermal vacuum switch at the thermostat housing controlled the vacuum direction in relation to the coolant temperature.

The Autolite/ Motorcraft distributor's weak link was this single shaft bushing. Because oil distribution to the bushing is decidedly poor, bushing wear tends to be severe. Shaft wobble causes point bounce and irregular ignition timing.

Breaker-plate function in these Ford distributors is dicey at best. The original factory breaker plate (left) worked quite well. Ford Motorcraft and aftermarket breaker plate replacements (center and right) tend to be terrible. They do not work smoothly and tend to weaken at the pivot point.

Expect to see two types of vacuum advance units for old Ford distributors. The early-style advance unit (left) is curved via shims and spring pressure. An aftermarket advance unit (right) can be adjusted with an Allen wrench through the vacuum port.

Beneath the breaker plate are the centrifugal advance weights and springs, which go to work as RPM increases. The flyweights work against spring pressure to control the rate of advance. Swapping springs of different tensions controls the rate of advance.

Ford's Duraspark ignition arrived in 1974 and has been an excellent, reliable factory ignition system. Both the vacuum and centrifugal advance mechanisms work the same way as the older Autolite distributors. This Duraspark distributor is 1979 vintage with the larger spread-post distributor cap that was designed to prevent crossfire. These wide caps and spacers can be retrofitted to earlier distributors as well.

Find true TDC at the number-1 cylinder, which should be midway in the crank rollover point for the crank journal. Install and index the distributor at the number-1 cylinder. This is static timing and where you begin tuning.

When you fire the engine, be ready to set ignition timing right off the bat with the engine at 2,500 to 3,500 rpm to learn total timing. With the vacuum advance connected at 3,500 rpm, where is your ignition timing? Ignition timing should be checked two ways at 2,500 to 3,500 rpm: with the vacuum advance connected and disconnected. Total ignition timing with the vacuum advance connected should be no more than 36 degrees BTDC. At idle, it should be around 6 to 12 degrees BTDC.

When dialing in total timing, begin conservatively (at 30 to 34 degrees BTDC) and observe operation. Push it as far as 36 to 38 degrees BTDC but go no higher. Under hard acceleration or loaded on a dyno, listen for spark knock. If you have spark knock, retard the ignition timing 1 degree at a time.

When checking ignition timing, not only do you want to know the total ignition timing (advance) but also the rate of advance when the throttle is opened. When the throttle is goosed, how quickly does spark advance occur? Does it occur too early at lower RPM, or is it slow to come on as the throttle is opened and RPM increases? You want spark advance to roll with the RPM increase and throttle movement. If you don't have a vacuum advance, spark advance should increase in linear fashion with RPM.

Conditions change when it is hot and you're roaring around a road course at wide-open throttle. This is when you can get pinging (spark knock) and not be able to hear it, which is when the damage gets done. This is why you want to begin conservatively with ignition timing and work it 1 degree at a time. Expected total timing also depends on the cam profile, octane rating, and induction.

Spark Knock

Spark knock, detonation, pinging, and preignition are all the same thing. Spark knock happens with early light-off, a red-hot piece of carbon or a ragged casting edge, overheating, too low of a fuel-octane rating, too high of compression, a cam profile with too much cylinder pressure or working compression, or the ambient air being too hot. The rattling or knocking that is heard is abnormal combustion that results in a strong shock wave across the piston dome, which acts on the piston pin and skirts, causing the metallic rattling sound that is heard under hard acceleration.

To eliminate spark knock, first establish why there is spark knock. What do you have for fuel octane and fuel mixture? Is the mixture too lean? Have you confirmed both static and working compression? Do you have carboned-up combustion chambers? What is the known cam profile? What is the ambient temperature?

Depending upon your initial findings, you can make spark timing adjustments, retarding total timing 1 degree at a time to see what comes under a load at wide-open throttle. Depending on other issues, you may eliminate spark knock but lose power.

Breaker-Point Ignition

Point-triggered, or breaker-point, ignition is a simple on/off switch that opens and closes the primary ignition circuit to charge up the coil and induce a brief discharge of high-energy current to fire a spark plug. When you turn on the ignition switch, power travels to the primary ignition circuit to energize the coil and breaker points. Current travels through a resistance wire in a Ford to the primary circuit. If the points are closed, the current flow across the contact points tends to burn the contacts. As current flows through the primary side of the ignition coil, it creates a strong magnetic field, which induces a huge surge of big-time current on the secondary side to the distributor.

The condenser is there to take up the surge of high-energy electricity that would arc violently across the open point gap if it wasn't for the condenser. This action would quickly burn and pit the contacts. However, there's more. The condenser allows the ignition system to build electrical momentum with a steady clip of 20,000 to 30,000 volts to the secondary side to fire the spark plugs.

The average garage mechanic will say that an engine will run without the condenser. However, engines generally don't run very well without condensers because the condenser acts as an electrical cushion, a shock absorber for high-energy electricity. Without it, electricity returns to ground, arcing across the points and being of little value to operation.

It is important to understand that the pink ignition-coil power lead is the resistance wire, which reduces voltage to the factory ignition coil. When going to an aftermarket ignition system, you need to bypass the pink resistor wire from the ignition switch, which is connected behind the dashboard at the main wiring loom or the ignition switch directly. Run a new lead from the ignition switch or main harness to the coil, which becomes energized when starting the engine.

Dwell Time

Ignition points are a rotary cam-actuated switch that operates in time with your engine's firing order. The opening and closing of points turn electricity on and off through the ignition coil. Dwell time is the amount of time that the distributor shaft rotates in degrees when the points are closed. Each time the points open, a spark plug fires.

With a dual-point distributor, dwell time is increased to build more coil saturation and a more potent spark. The limitations of a single set of ignition points are also eliminated. A key to improved performance is increased dwell time and a stronger spark. When the point gap is widened, dwell time is increased.

Electronic Ignition

Despite a point-triggered ignition's time-proven ability to fire spark plugs with precision accuracy, there are shortcomings. As engine speed is increased, there's less dwell time to build adequate current, which reduces spark potency. This causes misfire at high RPM because a powerful-enough spark to overcome high cylinder pressures is needed. At high RPM, points tend to bounce and flutter, which also causes misfire. This is where transistorized ignition came from to begin with (and later, Hall-effect electronic ignition). There has also been capacitive discharge ignition with a very potent spark triggered by ignition points.

Ford was among the first to use a transistorized ignition in the early 1960s. Duraspark did so in 1975. Chrysler was the first U.S. automaker to go with mass-production

Mallory's Unilite ignition really is the original aftermarket system. It offers solid reliability and is easy to install. Drop this unit right into your Ford distributor or invest in a Mallory Unilite distributor.

If you use a PerTronix Ignitor system, complement the Ignitor with the PerTronix 600 digital rev limiter. This is a nice safety feature to have because it keeps your engine out of trouble by setting a maximum rev limit. The digital microcontroller provides greater accuracy (+/-0.01 percent) over analog systems. Easy-to-use rotary switches permit settings with a resolution of 100 rpm. There's even a tachometer output with the TTL interface with a near 50-percent duty cycle.

electronic ignition in 1974. Somewhere in there was GM's first shot at mag-triggered electronic ignition and high-energy ignition (HEI) for the 1975 model year. HEI was a great idea because it eliminated the external ignition coil.

There have also been light-triggered electronic ignition systems

---

PerTronix offers the Second Strike multi-spark ignition amplifier. It is the only system to provide a second spark throughout the RPM range with a powerful capacitive discharge (CD) second spark, which results in more complete combustion. Increased burn time improves horsepower and torque at high RPM. In addition, it has a built-in rev limiter.

with shutter-wheel triggers and light-emitting diodes (LEDs), such as Mallory's Unilite ignition in the 1970s, which is still in production today. Light-triggered ignitions have performed very well and with great reliability. Most electronic ignition systems since the 1970s have been Hall-effect (magnetic trigger) systems, which are the most reliable. In fact, even in this age of coil-on-plug, fuel-injected engine-control systems, the Hall effect is still used in crank trigger capacity.

The main reason that automakers switched to electronic ignition in the 1970s wasn't so much for performance. They did so to reduce emissions because every misfire results in unburned hydrocarbons and increased emissions. If you listen to new cars and trucks today, they don't misfire. That comes from a potent high-energy spark and the precision of electronic fuel injection.

When combining electronic

The MSD 6AL box needs little introduction with performance enthusiasts. With less power draw and higher output, MSD lights the fire with microprocessors and updated circuits. Efficient components monitor and handle every firing and rev limit to produce more power while pulling less current.

ignition with capacitive discharge, it allows an inductive-type ignition system to build tremendous amounts of electricity for the secondary side to fire spark plugs. When you get right down to MSD's ignition boxes, that is exactly what they are but on a more high-tech scale. They pack a huge wallop and discharge huge amounts of electricity for each spark-plug firing. In fact, these systems are designed to handle up to 12,000 rpm, which small-block Ford engines will never see.

The key to performance and cleaner emissions is a potent spark. How that potent spark is achieved depends on the support system and what is used for spark enhancement. For example, MSD has a variety of ignition-enhancement systems, most of which are based on capacitive discharge. The MSD 6A series of ignition enhancers are all based on this principle, and they do an outstanding job of keeping the fire lit at high RPM. One MSD enhancer, the 6 Boost Timing Master (BTM) allows you to control spark timing if you're running a supercharger or nitrous

oxide. This helps you stay out of trouble when the heat gets hot and your foot is in it.

Ignition Coils

Most factory Ford ignition coils from the early 1970s make approximately 20,000 to 30,000 volts. This makes them less than adequate for high-performance use. Stock ignition coils work fine for normal driving at low- to mid-range RPM. However, when you start spinning a Ford small-block at 6,000 rpm or higher at wide-open throttle, the factory coil will not keep up. It will continue to fire the spark plugs, but it will not do so at the intensity that is required to light the mixture. This is a combination of dwell/saturation time and spark potency.

At high RPM under great cylinder pressures, a weak spark gets snuffed out, which hinders its ability to light

The MSD Blaster ignition coil is a productive drop-in replacement for the factory coil. This provides a hotter spark, which ensures a complete light-off at high RPM.

This Mallory coil with the HyFire Ignition and the ProMaster S/S provides 300 milliamps of electricity and a maximum output of 40,000 volts. It features an efficient winding design and assembly for a compact size. Primary and secondary windings are encased in polyurethane for durability.

This is a closer look at the original PerTronix Ignitor for Ford distributors. These modules endure (they last decades). Don't forget to reinstall the ground strap when installing any of the three Ignitor types. The Ignitor requires a 12-volt power supply from the ignition switch, which means bypassing the pink resistance wire.

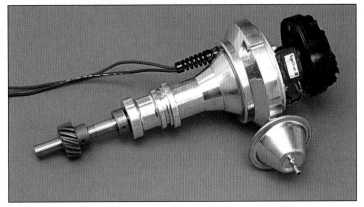

PerTronix not only makes ignition retrofits but also makes complete Ignitor distributors that drop right in place of the stock Autolite or Motorcraft ignition. These are high-quality 6061-T6 billet-aluminum housings with Ignitor II modules.

the mixture. If you add supercharging or nitrous oxide, it becomes overwhelmed quickly. Therefore, get a powerful ignition coil coupled with an ignition enhancer, such as capacitive or multi-spark discharge. You want the most spark that your ignition system can pack even with a street engine.

Distributor

The good news is that many small-block Ford distributor types are available. There's not much good to say about Ford distributors because they're just not up to the task of high-RPM use. The Autolite/ Motorcraft distributors consist of bronze bushings on a steel shaft. Some have only one bushing, and others having two. Because oil distribution is so poor, bushings and shafts wear out quickly, causing side play (wobble) and point bounce at high RPM. Unless you're building a stealthy stocker, avoid using Ford distributors.

If your small-block has been upgraded to Sniper EFI and you have no idea which ignition option is the best, check out Holley's Sniper EFI HyperSpark distributors. These good-looking billet distributors use a Hall-effect crank-signal sensor, which provides a noise-free RPM signal to the Sniper engine control unit (ECU). This easy plug-and-play system adds timing control and completes the Sniper EFI installation.

As with the Holley carburetors that were mentioned earlier in this book, I tend to go with what I know works. I know that components from MSD Ignition work without a hitch. The same can be said for ignition components from PerTronix,

The PerTronix Ignitor III is the most advanced of the Ignitor series. It offers multi-spark performance throughout all RPM ranges, an integrated digital rev limiter with LED feedback for precise RPM tuning, and a memory-safe function that stores settings and eliminates unintended changes to the rev limit. It also features adaptive dwell technology that maintains peak energy and virtually eliminates misfire.

Mallory, Crane, and Performance Distributors. These are exceptional systems. I've had good experiences with these ignition systems, and when they're installed and tuned properly, they offer outstanding performance.

The choice boils down to usage: street or race or a combination of both. Street engines should be equipped with a distributor that has a vacuum advance for good off-idle response. A street/strip combination leans toward a centrifugal-advance distributor, depending upon how much time is spent at high RPM. Again, how is your engine operated most of the time? This determines the type of distributor that you're going to choose.

MSD Ignition

There's a reason why MSD's name is so recognizable. It's because so much research and development go into its products. MSD's ignition

Street engines need the MSD Street Pro-Billet distributor with vacuum advance for good off-idle performance. The diameter of the special MSD cap and housing is 5/8 inch smaller than the diameter for Ford Duraspark distributors, which provides room at the front of the engine. I like the MSD cap, which features male terminals and is firmly screwed down to the cap.

products are tested in tough, grueling environments where they're subjected to the worst conditions imaginable.

Three basic choices are available for those who want to use an MSD distributor: billet, billet with a vacuum advance, and the electronic programmable units. For the street, use the MSD Pro-Billet distributor with a vacuum advance. This is a high-performance street distributor that has been engineered and manufactured for ease of use with an

The MSD Pro-Billet distributor incorporates MSD's race-proven magnetic pickup and precision reluctor to deliver accurate trigger signals to the external MSD Ignition box throughout high RPM. The reluctor assembly is turned by a hardened steel shaft that rides in a sealed ball bearing for high RPM stability and endurance.

easy to access and adjust mechanical advance and a vacuum advance that you can adjust with a simple Allen wrench. Mechanical advance is easy to tune because the advance is right under the rotor. It's a matter of changing spring tension and and/or bushings.

Mallory

Another name that has held its own through the years is Mallory, which has the same level of reliability and performance through Unilite technology. At least two Mallory Unilite ignitions are available

The Mallory Unilite ignition was introduced at a time when enthusiasts wanted precision performance and were tired of ignition points. Unilite became the standard for solid reliable electronic ignition systems. You can still get Unilite today from Mallory. It is that good. Go to holley.com for more detail.

for the small-block Ford: single- and dual-advance distributors with mechanical and vacuum advance, which are primarily for street use.

The Mallory HEI distributor is a coil-in-cap self-contained unit. Fitment may be tricky with the Mallory HEI, depending on your small-block's induction system. The HEI distributor can be converted for racing with an advance lockout. For those who tune your Mallory HEI, both mechanical and vacuum advances are programmable and easy to access.

The Mallory distributor is a mechanical-advance-only unit with Unilite for pinpoint accuracy. What makes the Mallory a great distributor is its reliability and maintenance-free operation. Aside from the occasional cap and rotor replacement or wiping the optics, it requires no attention. Use this distributor for high-RPM driving.

Performance Distributors

Performance Distributors in Memphis, Tennessee, is located within spitting distance of Comp Cams and enjoys a great reputation for building affordable high-quality ignition systems for Ford applications. Founded by the late Kelly Davis, Performance Distributors is still a family-owned-and-operated business. Talking on the phone with these folks is like chatting with an old friend.

For small-block Fords, two basic types of electronic ignition systems are available: Ford's time-proven Duraspark ignition and the revolutionary D.U.I. (Davis Unified Ignition), which is based on GM's HEI system with a self-contained ignition coil in cap. Either way, you get factory-style reliability and easy-to-get parts. If you want a stock appearance for your engine project, Performance Distributors is very helpful with the proven Duraspark. If you want a clean appearance without clutter, the D.U.I. system is

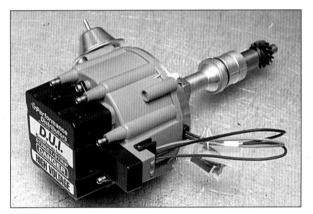

Steve Davis at Performance Distributors has been a longtime player in the ignition business. This company makes terrific ignition systems. The all-in-one D.U.I. (Davis Unified Ignition) takes GM's HEI ignition and applies it to Ford engines. No external coils, modules, or spark boxes are needed. Because of the size of the HEI design, make sure that you have clearance at the front of the engine.

Before installing a new distributor, make sure that you have the correct drive gear for your specific camshaft. Flat-tappet cams call for an iron gear. Roller cams call for a bronze or steel gear. Check the installed endplay (as shown), which should be 0.005 to 0.010 inch.

the best choice.

When ordering a Duraspark distributor from Performance Distributors, you're getting a custom-calibrated piece that has been curved for your application. That's why Performance Distributors wants to know all about your engine when you make an order. Performance Distributors blueprints every distributor with a full-length bronze bushing, new hard parts, and precision calibration for a seamless advance as RPM increases. Each Duraspark distributor is capable of 10,000 rpm, although I suggest not going there. Please specify that you want either a flat-tappet or roller camshaft with your order.

The racing D.U.I. system can handle up to 9,000 rpm. Because it delivers a greater dwell angle, it delivers a hotter spark, which enables you to widen the spark-plug gaps to 0.050 to 0.055 inch. Because these distributors are already curved to your custom application, you can just install and go.

Ignition Wires

Although many aftermarket ignition wires are available, I use what I know and what has worked well for me. MSD ignition wires stand up to extreme heat and get electricity swiftly to their destination. Because you can get MSD ignition wires in black as well as red, they render a more stock appearance if that's what you desire. MSD wires have an 8.5-mm outer extrusion that stands up to heat. Inside of this jacket is extra-heavy glass braid, a high-dielectric insulator, and a helically-wrapped copper alloy conductor. Inside of that is a ferro-magnetically impregnated core to get current to the spark plugs at Autobahn speed. Again, this is not a sales pitch. It is what has worked best

The Live Wires from Performance Distributor look good and are well insulated.

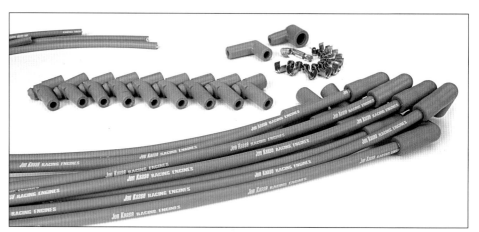

Jon Kaase Racing Engines produces these terrific heavily insulated racing ignition wires that resist heat and virtually never break down.

for me and for untold thousands of others.

It's not only about the spark plug leads that you choose but also how you route and locate them. Ignition wires should be routed parallel where possible at least 1/4 inch or more apart to minimize the risk of crossfire. Keep the wires at least 1/4 to 1/2 inch from metal surfaces to prevent arcing to ground and misfire. Crossfire, which is when a spark plug receives current that was intended for a different spark plug, can destroy

an engine at high RPM. Because high-energy electricity is very unpredictable, it travels unexpected paths at times and for reasons that we don't always understand.

You can have the most ironclad ignition system and experience stray current, crossfire, and a blown engine. Sometimes, current travels across exhaust gasses or even coolant in a water jacket, causing crossfire or misfire. This is why you must eliminate any potential future pitfalls during the build. Use the best ignition parts and set them up with the precision of an aircraft electrical system.

Regarding distributor caps and rotors, never buy these components based on an inexpensive price. Use those from companies with the best insulation and brass terminals, such as MSD, Accel, and Mallory, or use original equipment where possible. If you're committed to the use of a Ford distributor, opt for the Duraspark system. Use the Duraspark distributor cap with terminals spaced widely apart. Make sure that you have a vented cap to help keep ionized air levels to a minimum inside. With too much of an air gap between the rotor tip and terminal, you run the risk of crossfire inside the cap. Once your small-block has been in operation, monitor carbon tracking inside the cap, which can also cause crossfire and misfire.

Spark Plugs

Spark plugs have become a very complicated subject in recent years because there are so many different types. However, the best advice I can offer is to stick with what has worked for generations: the humble cross-electrode spark plug. Platinum-tip spark plugs work best with high-energy ignition systems because they last. Outside of that feature, stick with simple resistor or non-resistor spark plugs in your project.

Your greatest concern when selecting a spark plug is heat range. How quickly does your spark plug get rid of heat? If a spark plug's heat range is high, it doesn't get rid of heat quickly, which can cause spark knock. Even if there's no spark knock, the firing tip can run hotter than it should, causing premature failure.

Spark plugs can be a barometer for engine health. With older carbureted engines, the insulators should look tan with a minimum amount of deposits. These are "big ol' fat" Ford 18-mm, taper-fit spark plugs that were common on all Fords prior to 1975.

The heat range depends on how long the insulator is, which determines how quickly heat transfers to the cylinder head.

Ideally, your spark plug's heat range will keep combustion temperatures somewhere around 800°F to 1,500°F. The best indication of heat range depends on the spark plug insulator's color after a wide-open-throttle blast and shutdown. Tan to a light tan is what you want to see. Sooty black indicates that you're running too cold—not to mention rich. Snow white means that you are too lean and that heat range is too high. Small dots of aluminum on the insulator indicate bigger troubles, such as piston damage.

Heat range is also determined by the cam profile and how much cylinder pressure will be made as a result. Cylinder pressure is a product of dynamic or working compression, which affects spark-plug heat-range selection. Another issue to consider is how far the center electrode extends into the combustion chamber. Will it clear the piston? This can

be checked when you are checking valve-to-piston clearances during mock-up. This logic falls in line with heat-range selection. The longer the center electrode, the greater risk of piston contact. If your heads are already installed, this is something that you do carefully by slowly hand-cranking the engine, feeling for resistance, pulling the spark plug, and checking for contact.

Yet another item to consider is spark-plug indexing. Although some say that this doesn't matter, others live by it. Thread spark plugs where the anode (cross electrode) doesn't block the spark where the firing tip is open to the chamber. Mark each spark plug with a felt-tip marker and go for it.

Charging System

Small-block Fords were fitted with a variety of Autolite and Motorcraft alternators, both externally and internally regulated. Prior to 1965,

Powermaster alternators are available from a variety of performance retailers. This is the Autolite/Motorcraft 1G alternator for OEM-style installations. The maximum output is 65 amps.

The Motorcraft 3G alternator is a terrific high-output alternator and is a good drop-in replacement for both the 1G and 2G alternators.

If you use the externally regulated 1G alternator, use a solid-state voltage regulator from Motorcraft.

The 3G alternator can be used on a 5.0L engine with a serpentine belt or a V-belt (using a V-belt pulley). You can keep your factory external voltage regulator on the classics, but it will be out of the loop and inoperative.

these engines were fitted with generator charging systems, which are not addressed here. Although these charging systems were adequate in their day, they're not much to write home about today. If you are performing a concours restoration where authenticity is important, use a factory charging system. Some companies can restore a factory alternator with all of the correct markings and infuse more charging power in the process.

Several charging options are available. You can replace the factory alternator in a vintage Ford while keeping with its original look. These retro 1G externally regulated alternators make 75 amps, which is all that most vintage Fords, Mercurys, and Lincolns need. Reproduction Powermaster alternators conform to the proper size and appearance of original equipment while incorporating today's technology. They utilize OEM finishes and wiring connections for ease of installation and durability.

Ford's 2G alternator from the 1980s is never a good choice. It is known as the "fire starter" alternator because it tends to short out at the connector. Most engine builders with the 2G replace it with the advanced 3G or 4G alternator. The best option, of course, is a good internally regulated aftermarket alternator, such as the Ford 3G, which delivers a lot of power (up to 200 amps) without the hassle of those dated factory charging systems. The 3G Ford alternator is a simple one-wire alternator that you can easily adapt to any vehicle's electrical system. Painless Performance makes a kit that enables you to install a 3G or 4G single-wire alternator in a vintage externally regulated Ford, Mercury, or Lincoln.

This is the Motorcraft 2G alternator, which was original equipment on Fords in the 1980s. It is most commonly seen on 5.0L Mustangs. This was not one of Ford's better ideas because the connectors (arrows) can short and start a fire.

Starters

Small-block Ford engines were fitted with a direct-drive Autolite/Motorcraft starter until the early 1990s. It was a good serviceable starter for its time but is now out of date, especially if you build a high-compression small-block. That's when you need a modern, lightweight, high-torque, reduction-gear starter.

There are dozens of high-torque starters in the marketplace. With their gear-reduction drives, heavy-duty PowerMaster Mastertorque starters make the torque necessary (180 ft-lbs) to crank your small-block. They handle engines with compression ratios as high as 14.0:1. If the stock Motorcraft starter clears the oil pan, this mini starter will fit as well.

Invest in a high-quality proven starter solenoid. Some of the cheaper off-shore solenoids can stick and continue cranking the engine once it has started. One reason for sticking solenoids is overtightening the terminal nuts. They just need to be snug (not overtightened). Use the Ford solenoid in conjunction with the Powermaster's onboard solenoid for the best results.

TCI Automotive offers terrific high-torque starters for the small-block. The same goes for MSD, which offers a line of high-torque starters. If you're running long-tube headers or even shorties, protect the starter from destructive heat. Options are available for starter protection. Most of these aftermarket high-torque starters are fully adjustable to where you can adjust the index to suit the installation.

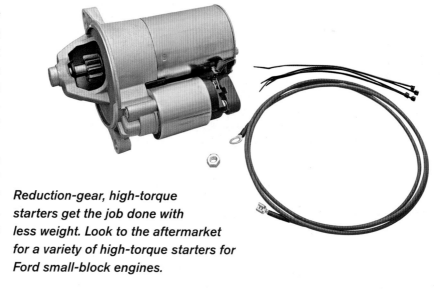

Reduction-gear, high-torque starters get the job done with less weight. Look to the aftermarket for a variety of high-torque starters for Ford small-block engines.

EXHAUST

The exhaust system and engine must work together. Headers and the exhaust system are just as important to power as induction, the camshaft profile, and cylinder heads.

While people think of induction, cylinder heads, cam profiles, compression, stroke, bore size, valve-spring pressures, carburetors and injectors, the throttle bore size, and the ignition system, some don't often consider the advantages of good exhaust scavenging. There's not much glamour with exhaust systems, aside from awe-inspiring sound.

Exhaust-System Sizing

The size of the primary tubes must meet the engine's requirements and the vehicle's intended use. Header-tube length and collector sizing must meet the maximum RPM requirements. Headers should fit the vehicle without ridiculous modifications. Displacement, horsepower output, average RPM, the vehicle's use most of the time, and any power-adders (nitrous oxide or supercharging) determine what's next.

What type of cylinder heads, bore and stroke, camshaft specifications (lobe centerline, exhaust opening, and lobe lift), rocker-arm ratio, port configuration, and exhaust-valve size are being used? What about the exhaust system? What type of pipe sizing, muffler type, and exit will be used?

A smaller primary tube diameter helps velocity, which enhances torque. A larger primary tube size is better for high RPM but hurts low- to mid-range torque. If header tubes are too small for the amount of power that the engine makes, this causes a restriction and makes the engine run hotter. If the header tubes are too large, torque is lost along with possible exhaust-gas reversion.

A small-block Ford is an air pump. It draws in cool air and atomized fuel, which are compressed and ignited to make power. Torque comes from velocity, meaning how fast cool

Long-tube headers deliver the greatest amount of power at high RPM. However, that's not all. Primary tube size affects not only horsepower but also low- to mid-range torque. These are large dyno primary tubes, which work well for high-RPM applications but sacrifice low-end power.

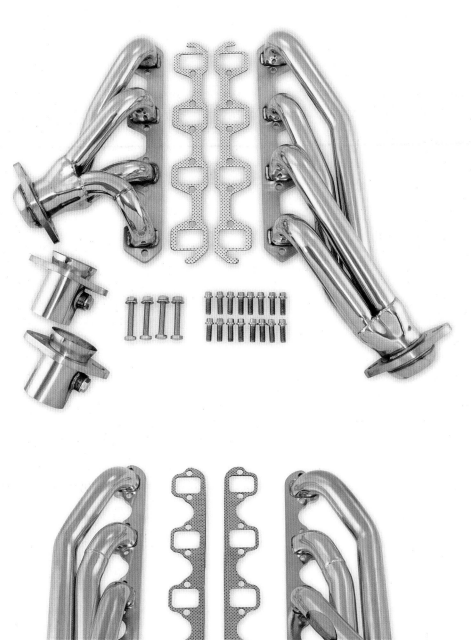

Shorty and semi-shorty headers offer a cleaner installation, but high-RPM power can be lost. Again, primary tube size matters. Go larger when seeking high-RPM horsepower. In addition, if you built a stroker and have greater displacement, greater primary tube sizing is necessary. These collectors have a provision for oxygen sensors for fuel-injected engines.

air and hot gasses can be moved through the engine. Horsepower at high RPM comes from the volume of air/fuel that can be moved through the engine. The faster that the air enters and exits the chambers, the more torque the engine will make. The larger the volume of air that is passed through the engine, the more horsepower the engine will make. Ideally, you have both.

You want deep breathing and scavenging throughout the RPM range from your small-block. With restriction comes excessive backpressure, the contamination of fresh air/fuel charges, and poor performance, depending upon the cam profile and RPM range that was expected. As RPM increases, the worse this phenomenon becomes because spent gasses tend to back up into the combustion chamber to contaminate the mixture. The more backwash that is on the intake stroke from spent gasses, the more contaminated the engine's chambers will become at high RPM.

Primary tube diameter and length are important considerations,

This is a very similar set of shorty headers that is void of the oxygen-sensor feature. The oxygen sensors may also be installed immediately after the header collectors. These headers have a ball-and-socket collector, which is preferred.

which can make it tricky to choose the right header for your application. With the knowledge of how primary tube size and length affect torque peak and below torque peak, you're ready to make an educated header purchase decision.

Here's a good formula for choosing the right headers for your application.

- Peak Torque RPM = primary tube size x 88,200 ÷ the displacement of one cylinder bore.
- Primary tube area = peak torque RPM ÷ 88,200 x displacement of one cylinder. Displacement of one cylinder is then multiplied by eight.
- Displacement of one cylinder = primary pipe area x 88,200 ÷ peak torque RPM.

The first two formulas provide a method for determining peak-torque RPM (as contributed by the primary pipes) if you have already selected headers and know engine size. The third formula applies where primary pipe area can be determined if the desired peak torque RPM and engine size are already known.

The MCE Raptor small-block displaces 427 ci, which calls for large primary tubes to handle the displacement and power. This is when a 351W becomes a huge 427-ci-displacement, 600-hp small-block with Hooker long-tube headers.

The JBA shorty headers from PerTronix deliver exceptional quality with mandrel-bent tubing and a ceramic coating for corrosion prevention. PerTronix follows the engine and bell with conformity to the point that you can install these headers prior to setting the engine.

Scott Drake has been reproducing 289 High Performance exhaust manifolds for decades. If you're building a stocker and want to improve exhaust scavenging, these are a good substitute for tubular headers, and they deliver a nice sound. Port-match these iron manifolds and improve scavenging.

Equal-length headers offer advantages if space is available. These advantages are explained in this chapter by the late Marlan Davis of Hot Rod magazine. The disadvantage is space. There's generally not enough room for equal-length headers, unless you're building an old-fashioned hot rod.

Here's a good formula from *Car Craft* magazine. While the example was from a 350-ci Chevrolet, this formula can be applied to a 302/351W Ford.

When you divide displacement (example being 350 ci) by eight cylinders, you end up with 43.75 ci per cylinder. Let's say that you want peak torque to come on board at about 4,000 rpm. Primary tube size choices are 1⅝, 1¾ and 1⅞ inches with a 0.040-inch wall thickness on average. That becomes 0.080 inch when you figure in 360 degrees of tube cross-section.

The formula looks like this:

$$Area =$$
$$(3.1416) \times (id\ radius) \times (id\ radius).$$
Through this formula you determine:
With 1⅝-inch tube,
you get 2.070 square inches.
With a 1¾-inch tube,
you get 2.190 square inches.
With a 1⅞-inch tube,
you get 2.530 square inches.

If you plug each of these values into the first equation, peak torque becomes 4,173 rpm; 4,416 rpm; and 5,100 rpm, respectively. This means that 1-5/8-inch primary tubes are optimal for this application. If you add displacement or want to push the RPM/horsepower ranges higher, you have to go up a size or two. Apply this formula to your 302/351W project.

An element that is not often addressed enough is primary tube length. Long-tube headers make more power, which is dyno proven. Shorty headers yield better fitment and don't take up as much room. However, they lose on the dyno compared to long-tube headers at high RPM.

Shorties offer easy installation compared to long-tube headers, and they're available in a variety of sizes for most popular Ford small-block applications. You get improved ground clearance, especially in tight installations, and shorties offer a definite improvement over factory manifolds. Most shorties bolt right to a factory exhaust system. Shorties suffer more restriction at the collector, which drives exhaust-gas temperatures skyward. Long-tube headers are clearly better for high-performance driving and power because they are designed specifically for racing and improved higher-RPM torque. They come in a greater number of sizes and lengths, especially for 289/302/351W engines.

The downsides to long-tube headers are that they're more challenging to install and they offer less clearance, especially in the Mustang, Cougar, Falcon, Comet, Fairlane, and Torino. They're easily damaged due to ground clearance, which means extra caution must be used when going over speed bumps. Often, long-tube headers will not clear your factory Ford starter, which means that you need a compact high-torque starter. One other issue with Ford compacts and intermediates is the power-steering control valve and ram, which may interfere with headers and pipes.

Secondary Tubes and Collectors

Secondary tubes and collectors have a like effect on torque peak. It comes down to secondary tube length coupled with diameter. Once you have established secondary tube length, you can then sort out size based on all of the elements mentioned earlier. This can get quite involved, but I am going to do my best to keep it simple.

Collectors and H-pipes/X-pipes affect torque production, but they don't affect horsepower as much. Drag racers, for example, don't sweat collector length much because it has little effect on horsepower, which is where drag racers live. However, if torque is important to you, collector size and length become very important.

Equal-Length, Step, and Tri-Y Headers

As if shorty and long-tube headers and pipe sizing weren't confusing enough, there's more to think about. Equal-length headers make fit a greater challenge with nearly any Ford V-8 engine. However, equal-length headers do serve a purpose. Equal-length headers are more effective with an open exhaust system at high RPM, but they make virtually no difference through mufflers on the street. Unless you intend to spin your big-block at high RPM through an open exhaust, equal-length headers make little sense.

Marlan Davis, technical editor at *Hot Rod* magazine, said, "When an engine's exhaust valve opens, there are two distinct movements within the exhaust pipe. The first is the pressure movement of the shock wave that is generated by the violent expansion of hot exhaust gas past the valve. This shock wave propagates through the gas in the pipe at a speed of 1,3002,000 ft/sec.

"The second movement is that of the exhaust-gas slug itself as it travels from the cylinder to the end of the pipe. The speed at which this slug travels is determined by the exhaust pipe's cross-sectional area and the

Ford began installing shorty headers on 1985 Mustangs that were equipped with 5.0L High Output roller-tappet power. It was a terrific model year for the legendary Fox Mustang LX and GT. Although factory tubular shorty headers were a great asset, there was also room for improvement. Check out the port size difference between Hedman shorties (bottom) and the Ford factory shorties (top).

Shorty-header installation is a whole lot easier than long-tube headers, where the vehicle must be jacked considerably high to get long-tube headers into the vehicle. This statement doesn't always apply to every vehicle. In some vehicles, long-tube headers can be dropped through the top.

engine's piston speed, but is usually about 200,300 ft/sec at the engine speed where maximum power is produced.

"When the shock wave reaches the pipe's open end and passes into the atmosphere, a rarefaction, or low-pressure wave, is reflected back up the pipe. If the pipe length is correctly adjusted at a given engine speed, this reflected low-pressure wave will arrive back at the exhaust valve during the valve-overlap period when both the intake and exhaust valves are open, in theory completely scavenging the cylinder of any residual gasses.

"Formulas exist to figure out the proper dimensions for a given application, but they're based on laboratory work under ideal conditions. For example, it's possible to determine theoretically the proper primary tube length to develop max torque at a given engine RPM, but such an optimized configuration for any given

speed may not produce the best overall results at other speeds (that is, yield the most area under the curve). Nevertheless, there are generally accepted header design principles."

Step headers, like their equal-length counterparts, are high-RPM/open-exhaust only if you are seeking significant results. The idea behind step headers is to create a

These Hedman shorties fit nicely and clear the strut towers of this 1989 Mustang GT. The best option is to use ceramic-coated headers, which contain the heat without it radiating into the engine compartment.

These custom Tri-Y headers were fabricated for a race-ready 351W stroker engine. You can have custom headers fabricated in nearly any major city in the United States, ranging from equal-length to step headers. Header fabrication work is expensive, but it's worth every penny if you're competing.

Stage 8's Grade-8 locking header fasteners don't come loose. They use a patented system that consists of a grooved hex-head bolt or nut, a retainer, and a snap clip. The retainer fits over the bolt head and locks the bolt against the header tube, and the snap clip holds the retainer in place.

Complete catalytic-converter H-pipe packages that are a direct bolt-in are available. This eliminates having to pay a local exhaust shop to fabricate them. This is an X-pipe cat package. X-pipes are available for conventional non-cat dual-exhaust systems.

broader, flatter torque curve. However, I personally have never seen any proof through actual dyno testing that this is true. Considering discussions that I've had with experienced engine builders, racers, and header manufacturers, the step header doesn't make enough of a difference in performance to warrant its cost. In theory, the step header is an interesting concept. In practical function, there's little to be gained from using them.

Tri-Y headers are most common with small-block Fords. The Tri-Y funnels hot exhaust pulses from four primary pipes into two and then into one collector. This approach creates a broader torque curve primarily for racing where you need grunt coming out of a turn into the straights. In other words, Tri-Ys provide better low- to mid-range torque. This happens by pairing cylinders that fire farthest apart to create a pulsing momentum with improved scavenging. This momentum creates velocity and, depending upon cam profile, draws out hot gasses while hauling in fresh air and fuel. The Tri-Y approach doesn't always work for all engines because its effectiveness is determined by the firing order.

Exhaust System Selection

As much as we've complained about noise ordinances in certain areas around the country, we're finding that noise just isn't what most people want anymore. Loud noise, no matter your age, causes deafness

Be careful when selecting an exhaust shop. While quality craftsmanship is required, some exhaust shops don't deliver it. Check the shop's reputation and its workmanship before committing.

For mainstream applications, such as a Mustang, Cougar, Fairlane, or Comet, simple bolt-on exhaust systems are available to use with stock or aftermarket mufflers.

and makes conversation impossible. On the open road at speed, a loud exhaust system can take a toll on your hearing, which is a very real concern.

Racers are learning that there's torque hidden in those exhaust silencers. Companies such as Flowmaster, Magnaflow, Hooker, JBA, Doug's, Borla, and others are also discovering more horsepower and torque through advanced muffler design and pipe-sizing technology. For the street, I like the Flowmaster Delta Flow Series 50 for throatiness and cabin quiet. The resonance and ringing in your ears are gone. The torque that you desire is here. These time-proven mufflers deliver real throat.

Summit Racing Equipment's website offers good information on

These aftermarket dual-exhaust systems (stock replacements) feature the correct brackets, hangers, and offsets to make installation easy. If your Ford was not originally equipped with a factory dual-exhaust system, the correct brackets and hangers are available to make the conversion.

The Flowmaster Delta Flow offers the best sound of any aftermarket muffler that I've heard. For tolerable cabin noise levels, the Series 50 Delta Flow delivers a throaty bark without overwhelming drone and resonance in the cabin.

how to design an exhaust system for your Ford muscle car. It first suggests knowing what size of pipe to choose once you get past the header collectors. Fortunately, the automotive aftermarket offers a huge variety of complete exhaust systems for all kinds of vintage Ford muscle cars, which makes selection and installation easier. Not all off-the-shelf systems out there are a great fit. In fact, you will probably need the expertise of a good exhaust shop to install just about any system because nearly all require some kind of adjustment to achieve proper fitment.

When shopping for an exhaust system, I suggest knowing the difference between a crush bend and mandrel bend, which affects exhaust flow. Crush bending causes flow restriction along the way. Mandrel bending provides a smooth journey for the exhaust, and it looks better. Always go with an H-pipe or X-pipe dual-exhaust system (balance tube) for improved scavenging and better sound. Without a balance tube, performance suffers, and you will end up with an exhaust system that sounds horrible.

National Parts Depot offers the most extensive line-up of exhaust systems for vintage Fords in the industry. You may combine these systems with a wide variety of aftermarket mufflers, depending upon the pipe size that is desired. Which muffler you choose for your small-block engine project depends on desired performance and noise levels. The key is to get your pipe sizing correct, and everything else will fall into place.

Complete aftermarket exhaust systems (stock replacement or performance) are available for late-model 1979–1993 Fox Body Mustangs.

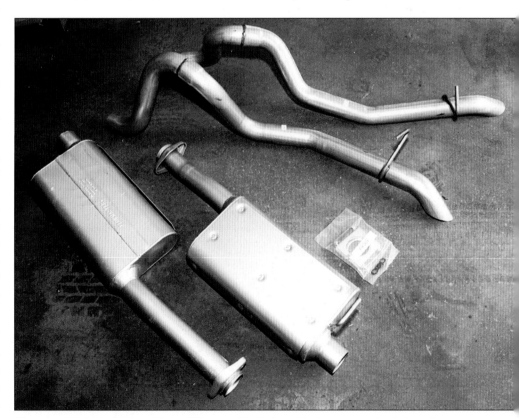

Flowmaster has Series 40 mufflers and tailpipes that are a perfect drop-in swap. Installation can be done in your home garage. Make sure to get the body high off the floor and onto quality jack stands. Never use a floor jack or hydraulic bottle jack by itself to support the vehicle.

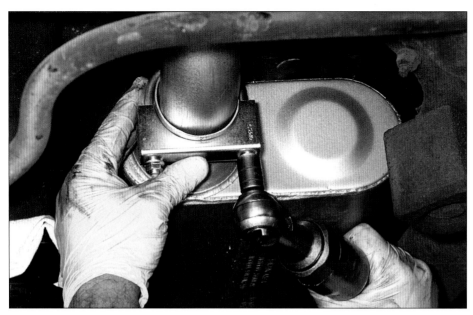

Flowmaster exhaust systems feature OEM–quality clamps and hardware.

Examine the muffler dimensions and pipe diameter/length. Measure the muffler body (end to end) along with the pipe ends. Aftermarket performance mufflers rarely have brackets like a stock muffler.

With aftermarket mufflers, you will have to hang them at the pipe.

Exhaust Pipe Sizing				
Pipe Diameter (Inches)	Pipe Area (Inches)	Total Estimated CFM	Maximum Horsepower Per Pipe	Maximum Horsepower for Dual Exhaust
1.50	1.48	171	78	155
1.75	2.07	239	108	217
2.00	2.76	318	144	289
2.25	3.55	408	185	371
2.50	4.43	509	232	463
2.75	5.41	622	283	566
3.00	6.49	747	339	679
3.25	7.67	882	401	802
3.50	8.59	1,029	468	935

(Table Courtesy exhaustvideos.com)

Based on the calculations, you should never need more than 3.000 inches of pipe diameter for a 600-hp 460. Remember, when you go too large, you lose torque, which is why you should keep pipe sizing conservative because larger isn't always better.

The best path to pipe selection is common sense. You don't need 3.000-inch pipes with a 350-hp engine. You can get away with 2½-inch-diameter pipes with a 400- to 500-hp small-block. Keep in mind how much space large-diameter pipes consume. It can be difficult to fit 2½- to 3-inch pipes underneath a Mustang or Torino.

The folks at exhaustvideos.com base their calculations on facts. They suggest that your engine needs to flow 1.5 cfm through the intake per 1 engine hp. The exhaust system needs to flow 2.5 cfm per 1 engine hp because hot gasses consume more space than cool incoming air. They suggest multiplying engine RPM by displacement and then dividing by 2. This is intake volume. When you take intake volume and figure in thermal expansion, this determines the exhaust gas volume. According to exhaustvideos.com, pipes typically handle 115 cfm per square inch.

Stainless or Aluminized?

Another item that people don't think about enough is material. Should you buy a stainless or aluminized steel exhaust system? Because exhaust systems are more a work of art these days than functional, additional thought must be given to material and aesthetics. Aluminized exhaust systems are more affordable but also more susceptible to rust as time passes, especially if you live where humidity is high.

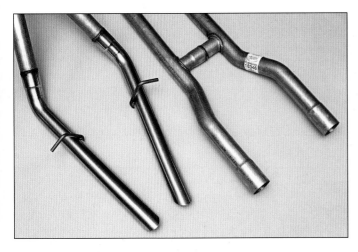

When ordering an exhaust system for a Fox Body Mustang, keep in mind the type of Fox Body Mustang that you have. Do you want chrome tips or to go without tips? Do you want turned-down exhaust or a straight pipe?

If appearance is important to you, you can ceramic coat the headers and pipes. However, it is very expensive. The beauty of ceramic coating is color choice, including a natural metal finish if you desire. Ceramic coatings, such as Jet Hot, can withstand temperatures up to 1,700°F. If you're going to dyno test a 429/460, remember that ceramic coating doesn't like the extreme heat of a dyno pull. It will fog badly. Dyno test with bare steel headers. Ceramic-coated headers are also available right out of the box, which eliminates the expense of having them coated.

If your budget allows, stainless steel is the best choice for an exhaust system because it will last the life of a restoration. Although stainless is corrosion resistant, it is not corrosion proof. It can rust in pinpoint locations if it is not cared for.

Not much attention is paid to exhaust tips, but they will affect performance to some degree, including sound. You want exhaust tips that are not restrictive, such as small quad-tips or louvered first-generation Mustang trumpet tips. Both are quite restrictive, although they're at the end of the system. While not an exact match, 2.5-inch aftermarket quad tips are available from various performance retailers.

H-Pipes and X-Pipes

Dual-exhaust systems must have a union where both banks interact with some uniformity. H-pipes and X-pipes are employed to balance the erratic pulses that occur on each bank of cylinders. Firing eight cylinders every 90 degrees in a 1-5-4-2-6-3-7-8 sequence is most surely a bizarre balancing act.

Since crankshaft counterweights and the flywheel/flexplate smooth out the pulses on the crankshaft, it's easy for most of us to forget that there are eight individual four-cycle combustion events going on every 720 degrees of crank rotation. This is a lot to think about.

The alternate firing sequences between the left and right banks means that there is a significant difference in exhaust-pressure pulses between each bank. This means that there is a backlog of exhaust molecules in one bank of cylinders when minimal backpressure is happening in the opposite bank. This is why automakers employ a balance tube between the two banks. This not only makes a difference in performance but also in sound.

Dual exhausts that are void of a balance tube sound horrible, with pop-gun pulses at the tailpipes. A balance tube softens the pulse and smooths out the action. With stone stockers, the balance tube equalizes exhaust gas backpressure while allowing exhaust gasses to flow smoothly from the tailpipes. The truth is that exhaust gas waves move in pulses instead of a smooth flow, which become more obvious when you step up cam attitude with increased duration. As these low and high exhaust pulses move through the exhaust system, they cruise through the pipes at different speeds. The exhaust crossover tube helps drive these pulses out into a more balanced pattern, which actually improves power and sound.

Enthusiasts ask, "Which is better—an H-pipe or an X-pipe?" Although X- and H-pipes offer better performance, each offers qualities that make it more suitable than the other. Selection depends upon what you want from your vehicle. We do know that each crossover tube nets different performance and sound. In my opinion, the H-pipe delivers a conventional V-8 sound—that throaty roar you're used to hearing at racetracks and cruises. The X-pipe delivers a more buzzy European sound with a hint of American V-8 in the throat.

It can be safely said the X-pipe makes little difference in power but more where power happens. H-pipes deliver power in the low and mid RPM ranges. You will get good low-end and medium range torque from the H-pipe. The X-pipe is more beneficial at high RPM where horsepower lives.

It also boils down to fitment. The H-pipe generally fits better than the X-pipe. Consider your transmission crossmember and floor pan before choosing the X-pipe.

ENGINE BUILDS

There's nothing quite like testing an engine in a dyno room, where myths and bench racing give way to the reality of raw physics and either pulse-quickening euphoria or hopeless despair.

Horsepower and torque don't come easily, and they surely don't come cheap. This chapter features a series of engine-build recipes that you are welcome to try out. Decide for yourself which build will work best for you or create your own formula for success.

Budget 347 Stroker

The Ford 347-ci stroker shows how much power you can get from a block that was originally engineered for 289/302 ci. You don't have to spend a fortune getting displacement into a street small-block. Fill 4.030/4.040-inch bores with 3.400 inches of stroke, and you have nearly 350 ci. With this increase in stroke comes a greater fuel and air charge plus the mechanical advantage of stroke. What's not to like about this?

The rod ratio and piston dwell time improves at each end of the bore to get real power. You want as much rod length as you can safely

fit into the bores. Engine builders all have different opinions about how to get power. The cheapest and quickest way to get power is with increased compression. It costs virtually nothing as long as you don't detonate the engine to death.

Horsepower is an element of speed. Torque is the grunt that gets

us there. If you're building a street engine, you need a broad torque curve and an engine that comes on strong from 2,500 rpm and keeps pulling to 5,500 rpm and ultimately peak horsepower around 6,000 to 6,500 rpm.

Mark Jeffrey of Trans-Am Racing likes engines with uniform amounts

Building a 347-ci stroker engine for street and weekend strip use does not have to be expensive. You can build a 500-hp, 347-ci stroker without breaking the bank by using more-affordable build techniques and parts.

Mark chose a late-model 5.0L roller block, which is a more rugged block than its vintage 289/302-ci predecessors. Avoid Ford blocks that were cast in the 1970s and early 1980s. They suffer from porosity and other weakness issues that make them vulnerable to failure. Build in strength by using ARP main studs and massaged two-bolt main caps.

Low-friction piston rings free up power that would otherwise be lost to internal friction. The downside to low-friction rings is longevity. Strong aftermarket I-beam rods and a cast-steel crank deliver plenty of strength for the horsepower and torque rating.

Mark is using an aggressive Comp Cams hydraulic roller cam—a custom grind with 232/232 duration, 0.550/0.550-inch lift, and 110-degree lobe centers.

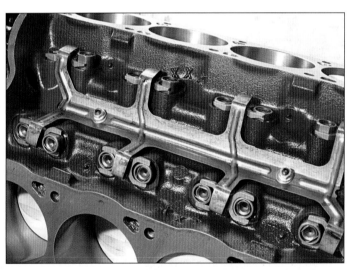

A conventional "spider" lifter and retainer setup is being used, which makes perfect sense with a roller block. This makes it easier to do a cam and lifter swap than if linked lifters were used.

of both horsepower and torque, which is good for the morning commute and up to the speed task on Saturday night. Jeffrey's budget 347 Street Demon is about torque for the street and horsepower for weekend racing and cruising. He does it with an affordable cast-steel crank, I-beam rods, and forged pistons. He has specified an aggressive street/strip hydraulic-roller cam from Comp Cams. Edelbrock Performer RPM cylinder heads with Air Gap induction and Holley carburetion on top complete the package.

Jeffrey's routine on Westech Performance Group's dyno has always been to try different things: timing adjustments, jet changes, cam and rocker-arm swaps, carburetor and manifold swaps, valve lash adjustments, and more. Jeffrey also understands that small header primary tubes can choke off horsepower.

This is Mark's own port-massaged Edelbrock Performer RPM cylinder head with 2.020/1.600-inch intake/exhaust valves, 60-cc chambers, and 160-cc intake-runner volumes.

The Performer RPM 60-cc, high-swirl chamber yields plenty of quench with a minimal amount of valve shrouding that would hurt flow.

Two different rocker-arm ratios are used on intake and exhaust valves to achieve appropriate lift values for each. These are the Trick Flow Specialties (part number 51400520) 1.7:1-ratio rocker arms and one-piece hardened pushrods (part number 21406400) on the exhaust side with the Comp 1.6:1-ratio Pro Magnums on the intake side.

Mark decided to experiment with both dual-plane and single-plane intake manifolds to compare the results. The dual-plane manifold provided better low- to mid-range torque. The single-plane manifold produced a pinch more horsepower but roughly the same amount of torque. Here, the Edelbrock Performer RPM Air Gap is great for low- to mid-range torque and high-RPM horsepower.

He knows that going too large can reduce backpressure and important mid-range torque. It is a matter of right-sizing the headers and exhaust pipes.

This 347 has a moderate compression ratio of 10.8:1 for use with 91-octane pump gas. Jeffrey has thermal-coated the pistons and valves to protect them from extreme heat. On the dyno, he found that the air/fuel ratio was lean at 13.9:1 to 14.2:1. Westech determined that he needed to go three jet sizes larger in the primaries. After performing two jet-check runs to verify the jet change, Westech brought the air/fuel ratio to a conservative 12.7:1.

Jeffrey switched from a dual-plane Edelbrock Performer RPM Air Gap to a single-plane Parker manifold to see

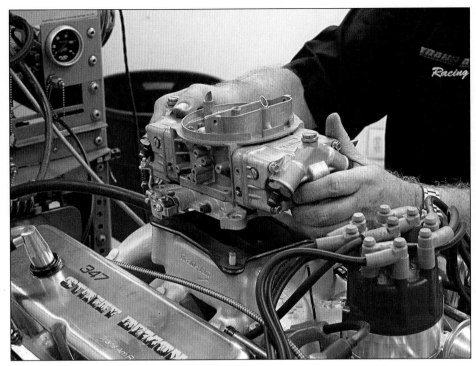

Mark used an 830-cfm Holley carburetor (part number 0-9381) for the 347 with the testing of both dual-plane and single-plane induction.

The Parker single-plane manifold yielded more high-RPM power and less low-end torque.

what would happen to power. The Parker single-plane, high-rise manifold has shorter runners, which adds horsepower at high RPM, but limits torque down low to mid-range. The Parker intake took peak horsepower from 485.2 to 495.1 at 6,500 rpm. He lost 8.9 ft-lbs of torque at 5,200 rpm. Not much was gained with the Parker.

Jeffrey's Westech dyno session began with peak horsepower at 479.2 at 6,500 rpm, with peak torque at 416.5 ft-lbs at 5,200 rpm. He tried rocker-arm swaps and the single-plane, high-rise manifold along with jet swaps to get 502.4 hp at 6,500 rpm, with peak torque at 425.1 ft-lbs at 5,200 rpm. That's not bad for a little small-block Ford with a lot of displacement.

Jeffrey said that peak torque should roll in at around 3,800 to 4,200 rpm with the dual-plane manifold. However, when that happens, peak horsepower isn't going to be 500. This is the reality of horsepower and torque because it is challenging to get both. What Jeffrey has learned from a simple 347 stroker is to focus on how the engine will be used most of the time.

With a milder hydraulic-roller cam, Edelbrock Performer RPM cylinder heads for 351W, the Performer RPM Air Gap, and 750- to 830-cfm carburetion, you can still get 400-plus hp at 6,000 rpm and good peak torque at 4,200 rpm along with durability. If you want real strip power, opt for a more aggressive hydraulic-roller cam and a single-plane manifold topped with 900-cfm carburetion.

Carroll Shelby's 427W

Most of us fondly remember racing legend and car builder Carroll Shelby. Shelby left an indelible mark

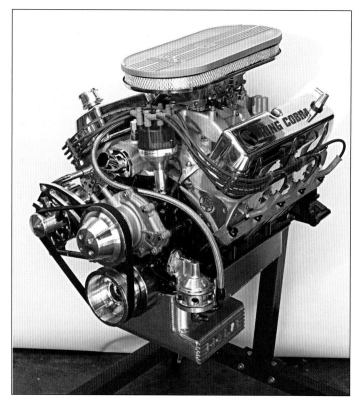

The late Carroll Shelby went to Mark Jeffrey of Trans-Am racing with an idea regarding what he wanted for his 1966 GT350 convertible. He and Mark brainstormed and came up with a 427-ci Windsor stroker powerhouse. It's good for street use and ready for the racetrack.

As with the 347 stroker, the Shelby 427W stroker gets main studs and a stud girdle for solid integrity. The 4.170-inch-stroke, forged-steel Scat crank can handle any power that Shelby can throw at it.

Because the 351W has a hardy iron block, Mark grabbed one off the shelf and went to work on refinements, such as notching the bores to clear the stroker rod bolts. The 351W block takes what was learned from the 289/302's weaknesses and has thicker main webs to handle the increased displacement.

on the auto industry to be remembered for generations, including his original vision of the two-seat, Ford-powered Cobra roadster in 1962, his refinements for the 1965 Mustang to conceive the GT350, and today's lightning-quick Shelby Mustang super-cars.

When I covered Shelby's 427-ci small-block build back in 2005, Shelby was 82 years old and as cantankerous as ever, with dozens of automotive marketing ideas to his

credit in more than 50 years in the business at that time. When I asked him how he would like to be remembered, his response was, "What the hell do I care? I'll be dead!"

When the opportunity arose to work with Trans-Am Racing on a 427W engine build for Carroll Shelby just up the street from Shelby's Gardena, California, shop, I jumped at the opportunity. I wanted to see just what the racing legend himself would choose as a list of ingredients for the

creation of a brutal-but-tolerable 351 Windsor stroker engine.

This engine was destined for Carroll's own personal 1966 Mustang GT350 continuation convertible that was built in the 1980s. Although the recipe is a tantalizing list that adds up to impressive performance, it is also a formula that you can use for your own vintage Ford 351W project. Shelby specified off-the-shelf aftermarket components that anyone could get from the aftermarket.

Nonetheless, more than 550 hp and 541 ft-lbs of torque isn't bad, considering what this formula could do for your ego. Considering the modest custom-camshaft grind, these eye-opening numbers impress and get your attention when the butterflies are pinned. Unmuffled on the Westech dyno, Shelby's 427W made 529 hp and 541 ft-lbs of torque. This was potentially a 600-hp engine.

Jeffrey's testing program at Westech included a ported Edelbrock Torker II single-plane intake and a slightly modified Edelbrock Performer RPM dual-plane intake. On top, a pair of performance carburetors were tried: a Pro Form atomizer and a 650 Mighty Demon.

Let's begin by looking at the components that Shelby decided to use in this streetable, race-able 550-hp small-block. Power comes from shoving a lot of displacement (427 ci) into the 1972-vintage 351W block, which worked well for Shelby with the Cobra.

Jeffrey opted for the pre-1982 offset-balance 28-ounce crank. Main journals were factory Ford dimensions. Rod journals were the 2.100-inch Chevy size with matching I-beam Scat connecting rods.

The 351W block is perfect for increased displacement upward of 430 ci, with right-sized main caps and thick main webs.

A stud girdle ties all main caps together and is bolstered with ARP main studs.

One of the challenges of using a stud girdle is clearance issues. The girdle needs to be modified to clear the oil pump (or the oil pump must be modified to clear) or cleared to clear the rod bolts.

Forged and coated 4.030-inch pistons are dished to control the increased stroke and the resulting increase in compression.

For Shelby's 427W, these forged and dished pistons worked fine to achieve a 10.7:1 compression ratio.

Jeffrey likes Cometic three-piece metal head gaskets. He opted for the 0.036-inch sandwiched pieces. This, of course, reduces detonation concerns when compression is as high on pump gas. Sealed Power moly rings and Clevite rod and main bearings take care of the reciprocating mass.

Edelbrock Victor Jr. cylinder heads were ported, the valves were enlarged, and custom seat angles were cut. Roger Helgesen, a cohort in crime with Jeffrey, took on the port work. A five-angle valve job for good flow added to the finishing touches, which delivered a whopping 312-cfm intake and 242-cfm exhaust. Out of the box, these heads flowed 275/204-cfm intake/exhaust.

The advantage of stroke is demonstrated here with forged dished pistons deep in their bores. A greater charge along with the mechanical advantage (leverage) of increased stroke is achieved. Aside from the stroke, you want the greatest rod ratio (longest rod) that you can safely fit into a 351W block.

Shelby went big for this 427W build. He opted for a Comp Cams hydraulic-roller cam with a duration of 246 degrees, with 0.585/0.595-inch intake/exhaust lift. The lobe separation is 112 degrees.

Mark chose a high-end dual-roller timing set and advanced the valve timing a few degrees.

Carroll Shelby was present for the dyno pull and was pleased with the numbers. Mark Jeffrey and Shelby were friends from the time that Mark was a boy. His father was in the jewelry business and knew Shelby personally.

Race-Ready Raptor 427W

Marvin McAfee of MCE Engines in Los Angeles, California, built powerful engines and was a street-racing legend back in the day. As McAfee entered his twilight, he wanted to go out with a bang. He conceived the Raptor 427W engine for a Mustang road-race car, but he didn't live long enough to see it completed.

Ford Performance provided the bones, an N351 race block, to make the Raptor happen. Summit Racing Equipment, Edelbrock, Eagle, Erson Cams, Holley, Performance Carburetors, Crane, ARP, and a host of others stepped up with the rest. McAfee knew what he wanted from this engine. He needed a block that could withstand 600 hp and the brutal demeanor of road racing. He believed that a stock 351W block wouldn't hold up to 550 to 600 hp and 6,500 to 7,500 rpm.

Ford Performance provided McAfee with an M-6010-N351 wet-sump block with 2.749-inch main journals, non-siamesed bores, thick nodular-iron main caps, heavy-duty webbing, semi-finished cylinder and lifter bores, thick decks, a 9.500-inch deck height, and a 4.000-4.030-inch bore range.

When McAfee was planning the Raptor, few believed that he could get past 500 hp with the Erson mechanical-roller cam that he had chosen. McAfee specified the Edelbrock/Glidden/Victor Pro-Port CNC cylinder head (part number 61099) in concert with the port-matched Super Victor intake (part number 2924). He said that valve selection was as critical as the cylinder heads that were chosen. Manley Performance went to work making custom-dimension valves for the Raptor. McAfee opted for hollow-stem stainless-steel valves instead of lightweight titanium, which would have been too expensive.

McAfee canvassed cam manufacturers for just the right combination of lift, duration, valve overlap, and lobe centers. He wanted something off the shelf that anyone could get. He found exactly what he was looking for at Erson Cams: a drag-racing profile that offered equal amounts of horsepower and torque. His strategy for power included internal friction reduction, reducing windage, improving oil-return flow (scavenging), working with valve timing, making finite adjustments to valve lash, and making improvements to the induction and exhaust. He wanted a liberal oil flow across the bearing journals yet insisted on a healthy oil wedge.

McAfee blueprinted the oil pump, checking all rotor clearances. He never installed anything right out of the box because he never trusted it. McAfee wanted at least 10 pounds of oil pressure for every 1,000 rpm along with plenty of volume with the engine hot.

McAfee always said that getting 600 hp was a no-brainer because true durability is what finishes races—not always power. A more aggressive cam grind will get you 600 hp. However, 600 hp isn't what McAfee envisioned with the Raptor. He expected 550 hp and 550 ft-lbs of torque with what he had planned. He knew that he needed torque for the turns and horsepower for the straightaways.

Extensive port and bowl work was performed on these race-ready

Glidden/Victor castings. In addition, he made what he believed was a common-sense valve selection for improved flow and minimal valve shrouding along with port matching to avoid airflow disruption.

The valves and seats must have a clean transition to keep turbulence to a minimum. This means using a valve-seat insert where there's no overhang or ragged edges (the pesky zones that disrupt airflow). Valve guides need to be out of the way where there's no turbulence around the stem. This is where good port and bowl work is crucial. Intake-manifold gaskets and ports must be right-sized where there's no turbulence generated as the air/fuel mixture passes from the manifold to the cylinder head. By the same token, you want clean exhaust passages where turbulence is kept to a minimum and scavenging is thorough.

Glidden/Victor Pro-Port Specifications	
Specifics	Description
Part Number	61099 bare
Combustion Chamber Volume	61 cc
Intake Runner Volume	280 cc
Exhaust Runner Volume	94 cc
Intake Valve Diameter	2.15 inches
Exhaust Valve Diameter	1.56 inches
Valve Stem Diameter	11/32 inch
Valve Type	Manley Hollow Stem Stainless Steel
Valve Guides	Manganese Bronze
Deck Thickness	5/8 inch
Valve Angle	15 degrees
Exhaust Port Location	2.5-inch spread, raised 0.520 inch
Spark Plug Fitment	14 mm x 3/4-inch reach with gasket seat

The Raptor block is a Ford Racing N351 casting with all of the nice benefits of a race block. This is a wet-sump block that could easily be adapted to dry-sump lubrication if necessary. Out of the crate, the N351 needed a lot of massaging.

From the beginning, the 427W Raptor from MCE Engines was planned as a road-race engine with 550 to 600 hp. It has a balance of horsepower and torque for the challenges of road racing: torque for the tight turns and horsepower for the straightaways.

Marvin cleaned the oil galleries to reduce fluid turbulence. The drainbacks in the valley were also cleaned and screened to keep contaminants out of the pan.

Forged pistons with low-friction rings are the key to gaining the power that is normally lost to internal friction. Marvin used his own special mix of assembly lube that is engineered for staying power and a wet start-up.

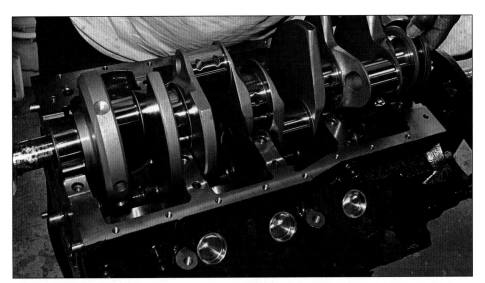

Marvin chose this knife-edged steel crank for his Raptor project along with H-beam rods and forged pistons with low-friction rings. Marvin ARP-studded the mains for extraordinary strength. Clearances must be checked in all directions before final assembly.

Erson Cam Specifications	
Specifics	**Description**
Part Number	E212991 with 1.050-inch (small) base circle
Grind Number	R-278-2 (intake/exhaust)
Lobe Separation	112 degrees +4
Lift	0.592 inch (intake/exhaust)
Advertised Duration	278/286 degrees (intake/exhaust)
Duration at 0.050 inch	238/246 degrees

Edelbrock invited McAfee to its research and development lab to give the Raptor a workout. A lot was learned from four dyno pulls. McAfee projected 550 hp along with comparable torque, which is exactly what he got. Engineers at Edelbrock were hoping for closer to 600, which would have taken a more aggressive cam. That was not McAfee's plan.

When building a road-race engine, you want a balance of horsepower and torque. After the first pull, McAfee learned that he needed larger 0.85 jets for the next pull to optimize the air/fuel ratio. Total advance remained at 36 degrees BTDC. The Raptor was finished making peak horsepower at 6,000 rpm. The most that Edelbrock and McAfee could get from this engine as it was built was 561 hp at 6,000 rpm and 540 ft-lbs of torque at 5,000 rpm. Jet swaps, timing adjustments, and two different 4150 Holleys didn't make any difference in these numbers.

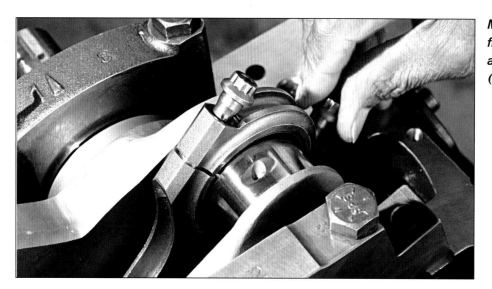

Marvin used the 4340 steel crankshaft from Probe Industries (part number 1002? along with 6.250-inch 4340 H-beam rods (part number 10082).

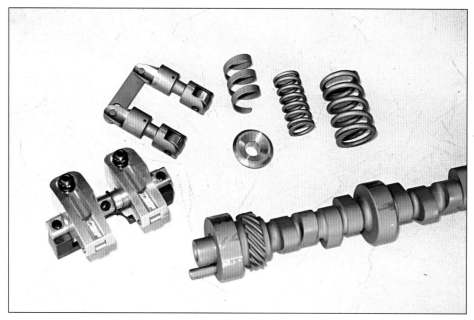

Erson Cams set up Marvin with the E212991 (part number R-278-2) small-base-circle mechanical cam with 0.592-inch valve lift, 278/286 degrees of advertised duration, and 238/246 degrees at 0.050 inch on 112-degree lobe centers. Some considered this to be an insufficient cam for this engine. In the end, Marvin got exactly what he wanted.

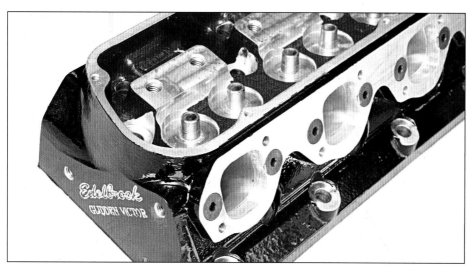

Edelbrock Glidden/Victor Jr. heads with port and bowl work courtesy of Edelbrock deliver the power. These castings have 2.150/1.560-inch intake/exhaust Manley custom valves and 61-cc chambers.

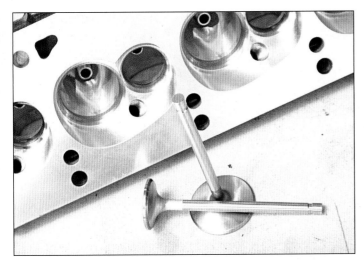

Among Edelbrock, Manley, and Marvin's own natural ability, these Glidden/Victor Jr. castings made uniform amounts of horsepower and torque. Had Marvin opted for a more aggressive cam profile, the Raptor would have produced more than 600 hp with comparable torque.

Edelbrock's 351W Super Victor was engineered for high-RPM horsepower, although a mild cam profile kept it from reaching 600 hp. Marvin chose a 2-inch carburetor spacer to get the carburetor farther away from engine heat and to increase velocity at the plenum.

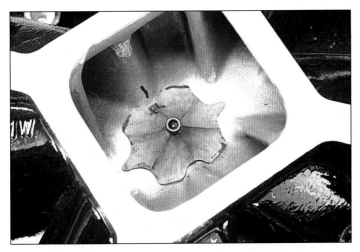

This epoxy-resin piece in the plenum was designed to smooth and vector airflow from the plenum to the runners.

The 1,000-cfm Holley Race Carburetor (part number 0-80513-1) with down-leg boosters was Marvin's first choice. MCE Engines had to dial in this carburetor for the 427W Raptor with the right 0.84/0.84 jetting to get started on the dyno. In the end, the jetting didn't make much of a difference in power.

Crane shaft-mounted, adjustable 1.6:1 rockers offer stability at high revs. The valve springs have Marvin's own special coating to reduce bind on start-up.

Performance Carburetors provided a 1,000-cfm Holley carburetor (part number 0-80514-1), which included a custom blueprint, down-leg boosters, and special modified metering blocks. By the time dyno testing was finished, both carburetors turned in the same numbers: about 560 hp and 540 ft-lbs of torque. Edelbrock's conclusion was that the Raptor needed more cam to reach 600 hp and 600 ft-lbs of torque.

5.0L High Output

Ford did performance enthusiasts a great service in 1985 with the roller-tappet 5.0L High Output V-8. It had a Holley 4180C 4-barrel carburetor and a Ford-tested engine block to manage the power.

Enthusiasts have done a lot with the roller-tappet block, with its thicker webs, cylinder walls, and deck, which enabled them to make outrageous amounts of power and keep this engine in one piece. Ford Performance (known as Ford Racing at the time) introduced a line of durable race blocks that we could take to the Moon. Performance only got better with help from Ford and the aftermarket in the 1990s, which led to the time slips that we currently enjoy.

Ford's venerable 1985–1993 5.0L High Output roller-tappet V-8 was a quantum leap in technology and power. The roller block has thick main webs, cylinder walls, and decks for durability. The automotive aftermarket has served this engine well by providing everything imaginable.

Gil Roiz found that his aging Fox Mustang's 5.0L engine was getting long in the tooth. He needed a fresh idea, and that was to build a new 5.0L High Output engine that could make 360 to 460 hp and be something that he could drive to work each day. He put together a plan to make 400 to 500 hp and 400 ft-lbs of torque at the crank.

Roiz looked to AFR for the cylinder heads, Crane Cams for the cam and valvetrain, Holley for induction, MSD for ignition, BBK Performance for innovative power adders, Fel-Pro for great gasket technology, ARP for the fasteners, and Summit Racing Equipment and Ford Performance for an assortment of speed parts. Eagle set up Roiz with an ESP armor-plated steel crank, H-beam rods, and Mahle forged pistons.

AFR's research and development lab went over the top, fine-tuning a pair of AFR 185 Renegade cylinder heads for Roiz's custom blueprinted 5.0L short-block. To get the compression that AFR wanted (10.67:1), it milled the heads to achieve 48-cc chambers. It then massaged the ports and chambers along with a nice custom valve job with 2.02/1.60-inch intake/exhaust valves. The 10.67:1 compression ratio was achieved with 0.041-inch thick Fel-Pro PermaTorque number-1135 head gaskets.

In 1985, Ford introduced its roller-tappet block, yielding strength and technology that was previously unmatched in small-block Ford history. The only block that was stronger was the Tunnel Port/Boss 302 block with its four-bolt mains and thicker webbing, decks, and cylinder walls. JGM Performance Engineering has installed ARP studs and performed all of the machine work.

Gil ordered Eagle's ESP Armor 4340 steel crank with a 3.000-inch stroke, H-beam rods, and coated Mahle forged flat-top pistons with valve reliefs large enough to clear those large 2.020-inch intake valves.

Crane Cams provided a nice grind with an off-the-shelf hydraulic roller (part number 44HR00217). It featured 110-degree lobe centers, 0.584/0.550-inch intake/exhaust, advertised duration at 0.050 inch (222/226), and triple springs (part number 96870).

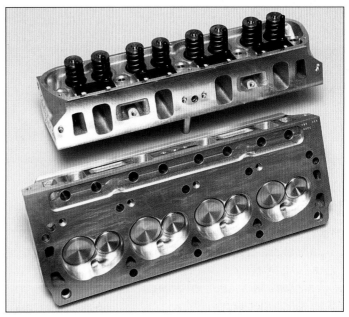

AFR (Air Flow Research) looked to its research-and-development lab for a pair of custom 185 Renegade cylinder heads for Gil's blueprinted 5.0L short-block. To get the compression desired (10.67:1), AFR milled the heads to get 48-cc combustion chambers, massaged the ports and chambers, and performed a custom valve job with 2.02/1.60-inch intake/exhaust valves.

AFR investigated what Crane had available and came up with a nice grind in an off-the-shelf hydraulic roller with 110-degree lobe centers (0.584/0.550-inch intake/exhaust, duration at 0.050-inch 222/226). For more valve lift, AFR suggested Crane Gold 1.7:1-ratio roller rockers along with single-piece, 0.080-inch-thick-wall, hardened pushrods. Getting onto the freeway, this 5.0L doesn't even break a sweat. The result was nearly 500 hp and 450 ft-lbs of torque.

For greater valve lift, Crane suggested its Gold 1.7:1-ratio roller rockers along with single-piece 0.080-inch-thick-wall hardened pushrods.

The Holley Systemax Induction (part number 300-72S) is shown with Ford Performance 24-pound injectors and a BBK 75-mm throttle body/EGR spacer for 1986–1993 5.0L High Output engines. These are EV6 injectors with Ford Performance's EV1 adaptor plugs.

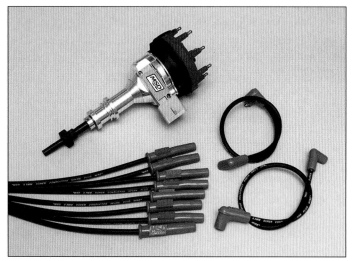

The MSD Thick Film Pro Billet Distributor is exactly what Gil wanted for this engine. It is complimented with the MSD 8.5-mm ignition wires, Blaster HVC ignition coil, and the MSD 6AL ignition box.

Street 302 Tunnel Port

Brent Lykins of Lykins Motorsports in Kentucky was building a Ford 1968 302-ci Tunnel Port small-block (one of very few left known to exist) and posted it online. I just naturally assumed that he was building this engine for the racetrack. However, it was being built for street use for one of his customers while another Tunnel Port was waiting in the wings for racing in need of critical parts that were nearly impossible to find.

"We're working with a Ford service replacement Boss 302 block," Lykins said. "This block had 4.060-inch bores when I got it, and it managed clean up at 4.070 inches. Mains were fitted with ARP main studs on the center fasteners, and the block was line honed.

"The decks were squared up, which was not a necessity because any 302 block from the era would have sufficed. The decks had been cut way low at some point in this block's service life. To restore proper geometry to the engine, I had custom pistons made so that they hung 0.020 inch out of the bores. To get our piston/head clearance back to the correct spot (0.039 to 0.040 inch), we used 0.060-inch-thick Cometic head gaskets.

"Durabond camshaft bearings were fitted to the block with Calico-coated Clevite main/rod bearings. Again, it's not a necessity, but in all my engine builds, whether street or race, we use coated bearings for an added measure. We opted for an Eagle cast-steel crankshaft with the 302's stock 3.000-inch stroke. Our Tunnel Port was fitted with Scat 5.400-inch I-beam rods, custom RaceTec pistons with valve reliefs specifically for the 302 Tunnel Port heads. These are flat-tops with a 1.5/1.5/3-mm ring pack. The compression ratio is 10.0:1.

"The camshaft is a Lykins Motorsports custom hydraulic roller (221/233 at 0.050 inch), which features 109-degree lobe centers and 0.625-inch lift with the 1.6:1 rocker ratio.

Ford's short-lived 302-ci 8V Tunnel Port was a 1968-only engine, and thank goodness for that. It was never installed in a production car and was conceived only for SCCA Trans-Am competition. Ford engineers reasoned that if the tunnel port worked well with the FE-series 427, it would also work well with the 302. It didn't.

The 302 Tunnel Port block (C8FE) became the Boss 302 block, which is exactly what this four-bolt main casting is. It is a production service replacement Boss block that Brent Lykins is using for his 302 Tunnel Port build for a customer. The block was already well used with 4.060-inch bores. He was able to clean them up to 4.070 inches.

Custom forged pistons and Scat 5.400-inch rods with low-friction rings are shown.

"As with any 'fat' intake port, a quick intake lobe is beneficial to snap the intake valve open. As with any older Ford intake/exhaust-port flow ratio, the typical 6-degree duration split that you see with most cams is nowhere near enough. Older heads favor valve overlap, and the added exhaust duration helps scavenge that big intake port.

"In the pan, we opted for a Melling M68A oil pump with an ARP pump shaft. The oil pan and pickup were custom pieces that featured a stock appearance on the outside with a trap door/baffle system on the inside.

"The harmonic balancer is an original 302 Tunnel Port balancer. No intake gaskets were available for the 302 Tunnel Port. I had to make intake gaskets from some gasket stock, which was easy to get. The intake manifold was vapor blasted for a nice original appearance.

"The distributor was a remanufactured off-the-shelf Motorcraft

To restore proper geometry to the engine, Brent had custom pistons made where they would be 0.020 inch out of the bores. To get piston/head clearances back to between 0.039 and 0.040 inch, Brent used a super-thick 0.060-inch Cometic head gasket. He's running a dual-roller timing set for precision timing and reduced friction.

distributor fitted with a steel distributor gear to match the roller camshaft, along with a PerTronix conversion. The Holley carburetors are classic-style 1850s that are 600 cfm each. They were restored and tuned by Drew Pojedinec in Georgia. A new progressive linkage was added. In the end, we made 386 hp at 6,600 rpm and 355 ft-lbs of torque."

These numbers make the Tunnel Port "square" in terms of horsepower and torque for weekend fun. Of course, a street Tunnel Port doesn't

The Tunnel Port's 58.6-cc chamber yields good quench, but it's really a terrible cylinder head, with 1.980/1.550-inch intake/exhaust valves. According to Brent, the flow numbers are 257/155 cfm (at best) at 0.700-inch valve lift.

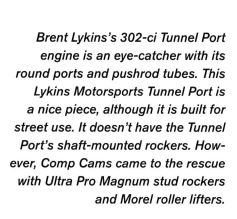

Brent Lykins's 302-ci Tunnel Port engine is an eye-catcher with its round ports and pushrod tubes. This Lykins Motorsports Tunnel Port is a nice piece, although it is built for street use. It doesn't have the Tunnel Port's shaft-mounted rockers. However, Comp Cams came to the rescue with Ultra Pro Magnum stud rockers and Morel roller lifters.

net much more than bragging rights but makes for great conversation on cruise night. Lykins said that he has another Tunnel Port engine from this customer waiting to be built.

Supercharged 347 Stroker

You can go way beyond what I've presented to you here, such as Richard Holdener's supercharged 347-ci stroker from Demon Engines. Because Holdener knows how to massage power from a small-block Ford, he went to work on the dyno, taking a nicely architected 347 to the next level.

"The idea behind this test was to demonstrate why it is important to combine these upgrades with boost. I mean, can't you just crank up the boost to make more power?" Holdener wrote on Summit Racing's OnAllCylinders website. "In reality, the best way to make boosted power is to increase the power output of the naturally aspirated motor before adding the boost. The benefit of this, especially on our supercharged combo, is that the modifications simultaneously increase the power while decreasing the boost.

"Wait, how exactly is that possible, making more power with less boost? Is it some sort of voodoo magic? No, it's just science, and it's especially desirable when running on pump gas."

This well-thought-out small-block has the benefits of increased stroke. It also has 5.400-inch Speedmaster rods for improved rod ratio along with the XFI cam profile from Comp.

Holdener began with E7TE iron heads, a factory hydraulic roller, GT40 induction, and a FAST XFI management system. He made 307 hp at 4,700 rpm and 401 ft-lbs of torque at

Richard Holdener chose to start with the basics of power with a naturally aspirated small-block and build power from there. Once maximum power and durability are achieved from the package, it's time to supercharge.

3,300 rpm. That's warmed up, but it's not going to impress anyone. Holdener then added a Vortech S-Trim supercharger with a 3.800-inch pulley and 6.750-inch crank pulley to go with a 3.45:1 internal Vortech gearing change to get 8 psi of boost at 5,700 rpm. These changes got Holdener 412 hp at 5,500 rpm and 462 ft-lbs of torque at 4,200 rpm.

For the next pull, he opted for Racing Head Service (RHS) un-ported head castings (274 cfm at 0.600 inch and 190 cfm at 0.600 inch) and a more robust XFI grind from Comp. The single-pattern cam has 0.579-inch lift, a dual-duration pattern of 236/246 at 0.050 inch, and an

LSA of 114 degrees. On top, Holdener selected Edelbrock's RPM II intake manifold to make a naturally aspirated 448 hp and 420 ft-lbs of torque.

For the last pull, Holdener went back to forced induction with the Vortech, reduced boost by 1.4 pounds, and made 665 hp at 6,300 rpm with torque coming on strong at 559 ft-lbs at 5,500 rpm.

"The only thing stopping this combination from topping 700 hp was fuel, as we were nowhere near the limit of the available blower speed," Holdener wrote on Summit Racing's OnAllCylinders website. "Looking back, the 36-pound injectors were a bad choice for our big-boy blower motor, as we quickly used up all the available fuel flow. The power and boost were still rising at our shut-off point, but this was already a lot of power for a stock 5.0L block."

5.0L Turbo Power

Turbocharging also creates more power. It just takes a little more infrastructure to make it happen. Holdener decided to experiment with a stock roller-tappet 5.0L High Output crate engine from BluePrint Engines (BPE) for his turbo project. He had concerns about boost and the durability of Ford's 5.0L roller block.

"The reason for the concern on a factory 5.0L application is that boost from almost any turbo or supercharger can push the power limit well past the breaking point of the production block," Holdener wrote as an article on *MotorTrend*'s website. "These blocks tend to crack from the main webbing up to the cam-bearing housings."

However, Holdener describes how to do it safely.

"For this project, we had a local muffler shop build the necessary tubing required to connect our stock exhaust manifolds to the existing Y-pipe," Holdener wrote. "That's right, I said *stock* exhaust manifolds—as in tubular, restrictive, factory 5.0L High Output manifolds."

"Little did I know that these same crimped headers could serve as effectively as turbo manifolds. For our system, we chose to combine the stock manifolds with a super cheap eBay turbo. Purchased for just $163, the GT-45-style turbo was capable of 800 hp (more than we ever hoped to see with the 5.0L). The problem is not one of power, as the torque production seems to be what splits the stock blocks."

Holdener opted for CNC-ported 205 aluminum heads from BPE. These ported castings feature 62-cc machined chambers and whopping 2.080/1.600-inch valves. He chose 1.6:1 Comp roller rockers. To see if his combination of stock tubular shorty headers, a cheap turbo from eBay,

Turbocharging is more involved than supercharging. However, here is an easy way to get there with low-buck, off-the-shelf components and modifications to prove that it makes power.

and monkey-motion muffler-shop plumbing would work, he installed the DIY turbo system on his stock 5.0L crate test mule. These heads were joined by a Comp XE274HR cam and a Trick Flow Street Burner intake.

To establish a baseline, Holdener started out with this engine naturally aspirated to see what it would do using 80-pound Accel injectors, a 70-mm Accufab throttle body, and Hooker headers. The engine made 386 hp and 374 ft-lbs of torque. He then went to work installing the eBay turbo along with an air-to-water ProCharger intercooler. An oil drain-back had to be installed in the pan. The first run netted 549 hp and 555 ft-lbs of torque with 7.8 pounds of boost from the low-budget turbo conversion.

The T4, GT-45 turbocharger yielded a 50-trim compressor wheel with a 0.66 area over radius (A/R), 68.9-mm inducer and 98-mm exducer. On the turbine side, it was equipped with a 1.05 A/R, 88-mm inducer and 77.5-mm exducer. The turbine side was set up to accept a 3.5-inch exhaust using the cast V-band flange. Holdener wrote that it is possible to use a less-expensive wastegate. However, he prefers to spend his money on a good boost controller. He went with a pair of 45-mm Gen-V wastegates from Turbosmart. Dual wastegates were unnecessary on such a mild turbo build.

"The turbo was configured with a 3.5-inch, single exhaust," Holdener wrote in the article. "We made sure to equip the exhaust tubing with a provision for the oxygen sensor. Equipped with the DIY turbo kit, we ran the boost up to a maximum of 7.8 psi (at the power peak). The result was an increase from 386 hp and 374 ft-lbs of torque to 549 hp and 555 ft-lbs of torque."

Holdener said that the cheap eBay turbo had more to give, but he thought that it was best to stop there with the knowledge that his plateau of torque near 550 ft-lbs was well within block-splitting territory. It appears that stock tubular exhaust manifolds flow enough to where you can forget all of the fancy power adding. He stressed that you must get all the exhaust to the turbo, control the boost, and get the tune spot on.

Air Flow Research
661-257-8124
airflowresearch.com

Automotive Racing Products (ARP)
800-826-3045
805-339-2200
arp-bolts.com

BBK Performance
951-296-1771
bbkperformance.com

Comp Cams
800-999-0853
901-795-2400
compcams.com

Crane Cams
866-388-5120
386-310-4875
cranecams.com

Eagle Specialty Products, Inc.
662-796-7373
eaglerod.com

Edelbrock Corporation
800-416-8628
310-781-2222 (Tech line only)
edelbrock.com

Federal-Mogul
Speed Pro/Sealed Power/Fel-Pro
248-354-7700
federalmogul.com

Holley Performance Products
270-782-2900
270-781-9741
holley.com

Jesel
732-901-1800
jesel.com

JGM Performance Engineering
661-257-0101

KB Pistons/Silv-O-Lite/Icon Forged
  Racing Pistons
United Engine & Machine Company
800-648-7970
775-882-7790
kb-silvolite.com

Lykins Motorsports
502-759-1431
lykinsmotorsports.com

Mahle/Clevite
mahle.com

Melling Engine Parts
517-787-8172
melling.com

Milodon
805-577-5970
milodon.com

MSD Ignition
915-857-5200
msdignition.com

Mustangs Etc.
818-787-7634
mustangsetc.com

Summit Racing Equipment
800-230-3030
330-630-3030
summitracing.com

Survival Motorsports
248-366-3309
248-931-0358 (After Hours Cell)
survivalmotorsports.com

Trick Flow Specialties
888-841-6556
330-630-1555
trickflow.com